RELENTLESS, TOO!

A 40 DAY JOURNEY FOR KIDS

By:
Charles Redding, Ph.D.

www.xulonpress.com

Endorsements

I wish I had this valuable resource when we were raising our children. The Church encourages parents to have daily devotionals with their children, but there are so few really good resources to help parents in this experience. Redding, an expert in family and children's ministry, has written a 40-day spiritual walk through Psalm 119. Each day there is a morning devotional and an evening prayer. His stories will capture the attention of your child. Both parents and children will profit from this sacred experience. Simple to read and observe, I'll be sharing *Relentless, Too!* with my grandchildren.

–Daryl Eldridge, Ph.D., author, speaker, educator, and president and cofounder of Rockbridge Seminary

God has blessed Charles Redding with a gift of moving kids toward Christ. He understands them and how to get them excited about Jesus. It was through his ministry that our daughter made her decision to follow Jesus. *Relentless, Too!* is an excellent resource for parents to lead their kids closer to Christ!

–Allen James, Pastor–Knoxville, Tennessee

Dr. Redding has written an excellent devotional guide taking children through the 176 verses of Psalm 119. *Relentless, Too!* helps children understand the richness of this chapter. Each day Redding uses one, two, or three verses with an interesting devotional for children to read in the morning. And they end their day by reading a few more verses and a prayer written by the author. For 40 days a child begins their day in the word and ends their day in the word. Thank you, Dr. Redding, for your superb work for children and families.

–Karen Kennemur, Ph.D., Associate Professor of Children's Ministry, Southwestern Baptist Theological Seminary

Charles Redding's book, *Relentless, Too!*, is exactly what every parent needs to enable them to have a meaningful, brief devotional with their children. Charles breaks God's word into a child's everyday language and uses real life examples to which they can relate. This book is a "must have" as you begin to shape your child's heart for Christ.

–D'Ann Laywell, Ph.D., Minister to Children, North Richland Hills Baptist Church

Introduction

Dear Parent,

This book, ***Relentless, Too!***, was written for your child. This book came about when my pastor, Kevin Moore, came to me and said he was writing a 40 day devotional book for adults on Psalm 119, entitled ***Relentless***. He then asked if I would write a companion book for children. What you now hold in your hand is the culmination of that project.

It was designed for individual use, small group use, or for an entire church to use at the same time. The children's book tracks verse by verse along with the adult version so that families and churches can experience Psalm 119 together. Imagine people of all ages passionately, relentlessly, pursuing Christ at the same time.

You will notice a morning devotion and an evening prayer are included for each of the 40 days. This is a recommendation; however, use it in the way that works best for your family. The important thing is to get your child into God's Word on a daily basis. My prayer is that your child will be forever changed after his or her 40 day journey through Psalm 119, and that your child will relentlessly pursue God and His Word all the days of his or her life.

Charles Redding

Day 1:

"Real Blessing"

Blessed are those whose ways are blameless,
who walk according to the law of the Lord.
Blessed are those who keep his testimonies,
with all of their heart they seek him.
Psalm 119:1-2

I love to get presents! Large ones, small ones, and in-between sized ones. You, too? I thought so. I like presents that do something or, better yet, have me do something. Once I was given a kaleidoscope. I would hold it up and look into the eyepiece. Immediately, I would see a beautiful colorful design. As I turned the end, I would see an ever-changing, breathtaking display of art. No two images were ever the same. What fun! Another time, I got one of those color by number books where you don't know what is hiding in the picture until you follow the instructions and color by the numbers. When I followed the directions, I discovered a dense jungle with a beautiful macaw!

Did you know the Bible is like that? God's Word says that people whose ways are blameless and who walk according to the Law of the Lord will be blessed. What does being "blessed" mean? I'm glad you asked! Being blessed can mean many things and God's blessings come in many forms. It could be something God does for you or it could be something God gives you. Either way, it is something wonderful that comes to you from God – like a present! Do God's blessings come to us wrapped up with a giant bow on top? Well, no, but it is still something great!

So, how do we get God's blessings? Good question. I know that at school if you turn in all your homework, don't run in the hallway, and raise your hand before blurting out the answer, the teacher is usually happy and you might get a smiley face. Does God work that way, too? No, not really.

Psalm 119:1-2 says God is looking for people who are following His Laws, and who are seeking Him with all their hearts. Those are the people God wants to bless: people who love Him so much, they want to do everything He wants them to do. I want to be one of those people! I love God and I want to keep His Laws and follow His ways. You, too? Great!

We are beginning a journey together to follow God and seek Him with our whole heart. We're going to do it together! As you begin your day today, be kind, fair, friendly and helpful; do all the other things you know God wants you to do, too. When you do wrong, tell God you're sorry. Ask Him to forgive you. As we go along, we will learn other things you can do to *"walk according to the Law of the Lord."* It's time to get going now. Have a great day!

Prayer: "Exceeding Obedience"

They also do no wrong; they walk in his ways. You have commanded your precepts to be kept exceedingly.
Psalm 119:3-4

Dear God, too often I do my own thing. I do what I want to do and don't give any thought to what you want me to do or about doing things your way. You command us, which means you give us very clear directions to follow and expect us to obey. You expect <u>me</u> to obey – very much – completely – every time the first time. Wow. God, I realize now that I miss the bull's-eye a lot. Please forgive me. Thank you that your forgiveness is mine because of what Jesus did on the cross. Help me to sleep in sweet peace tonight knowing I have your forgiveness. Help me begin my day tomorrow looking forward to all you are going to teach me through your Word. Thank you for the blessings I will receive as I seek you with all my heart.

Day 2:

"Oh that My Ways. . ."

Oh that my ways may be established to keep your statutes.
Then I would not be ashamed when I consider
all of your commandments.
Psalm 119:5-6

"Antonio, it's time for you and Carter to stop the video game and get on your homework," Mom called from downstairs. "Carter's mom will be here in an hour to pick him up." Antonio looked at Carter who shook his head and whispered, "Tell her we didn't have any homework." Antonio never lied to his mom, but they wanted to keep playing. Antonio whispered back, "What will we do tomorrow when it's time to turn it in?" "We'll just say we lost it. Willis and I do it all the time and never get caught. Just do it!" hissed Carter. Antonio wasn't sure, but he really wanted to play, so he lied. Antonio thought to himself, "I can do it later." The boys played until Carter's mom came. When Mom closed the door, she said, "Dinner's ready! Wash up and come to the table." After dinner and a bath, Mom read a book with him and sent him up to bed. He flopped on his bed and went right to sleep, never thinking again about the unfinished homework.

The next day in school, it was nearly lunchtime when the teacher said, "turn in your homework and line up". Instantly, Antonio thought about the homework, how he had lied to Mom, hadn't done his work, and was now in a real mess. He glanced over at Carter who just smiled and said, "Mrs. Ryan, I can't find my homework. I did it last night, but it's not in my folder." Antonio was feeling sick and so ashamed. He knew it was wrong to lie, and now Carter was expecting him to lie again to cover up the last lie. Antonio knew his mom would be very upset. He wished he had obeyed her yesterday and turned off the video game. No game was worth this.

There are several things Antonio could have done differently that could have changed the situation. Antonio knew that Carter tells lies. Yet, Antonio continued to spend lots of time with Carter – on the playground, after school and at home. What if Antonio had chosen to be friends with and to spend time with kids who obey? There were other kids in his class and in his neighborhood who seemed to make good choices and were never in trouble at school. What if he had chosen to be friends with those kids? 1 Corinthians 15:33 says, "Bad company corrupts good character." That means we begin acting like the people we hang around. The more we're with them, the more like them we become.

Would Antonio's situation have been different if he had said, "Okay, Mom" when his mom told him to turn off the video game and start his homework? Absolutely! Psalm 119:60 says, "I will hasten and not delay to obey your commands." The psalmist was saying, "God, when you give me a command, I will hurry up and do it as quickly as possible." If Antonio had done that with his mom's command, he would have avoided the shame and misery of his actions. When we obey God's Word and all His commands, we avoid misery and shame. When we choose to disobey God's commands, we always feel ashamed and need to ask for His forgiveness. Hurrying up to obey God's commands is always best. When you choose to obey God, He will help establish your life of obedience. Since God promises to never leave us and never to forsake us in Joshua 1:5, it means God is always with us helping us to obey.

So what can you do? First, choose carefully who you spend time with. Do your friends at school and in your neighborhood hurry up and obey the first time – every time? Or do they sometimes cheat and lie to get what they want? Choose friends who love God and do what He says. Choose friends who obey their parents and their teachers. Choose friends who do their homework and turn it in. Choose friends who don't lie and cheat. Listen to God and obey His commands that you find in His Word. He's right with you today. Follow Him.

Prayer: "Joy in Learning"

I will praise you with an upright heart
as I learn your righteous judgments.
I will keep your statutes; do not totally forsake me.
Psalm 119:7-8

I praise you, God, and thank you for helping me through my day. Help me to continue to learn your righteous judgments. Help me to follow your ways and keep your commands. Help me to grow to be the person you want me to be. Help me to rest in you tonight. In Jesus' name, Amen.

Day 3:

"The Pure Way"

How can a young man keep his way pure?
By keeping it according to your word.
With all of my heart I have sought you;
do not let me stray from your commandments.
Psalm 119:9-10

Once upon a time, there was a candy maker named Luigi Looterelli. Luigi owned a tiny little candy shop called "Looterelli's". His tiny candy shop perched on the corner of two very busy streets in his tiny little town. Luigi's tiny little town clung to the side of a not-so-tiny mountain like moss clung to the side of the trees on the side of that mountain.

The Looterellis were famous all across the land–from the highlands to the seashore–for their Easter candy. The secret recipe for these Easter delicacies had been handed down through the Looterelli family from generation to generation to generation. Finally, the recipe had been passed to Luigi. This would be the first year for Luigi to be responsible for carrying on the family tradition: to make the best Easter candy in the land, to uphold the honor of all the Looterelli family members who had gone before, and to keep the business strong to pass on to his children after him.

When Easter rolled around, crowds lined up and blocked both of the busy streets waiting to buy the famous

Looterelli treats. On Easter morning, excited boys and girls all over the land opened up their Looterelli Easter candy only to discover a shocking surprise – the candy tasted terrible! What could have happened? What could have gone wrong? Luigi had been very careful to follow the recipe. He measured everything. He cooked it just the right amount of time. He even bought brand new bowls to mix it in. What could possibly be the reason for this incredible tragedy? Oh wait, what's this? A note is scrawled across the bottom of the recipe – half covered with flour. "Let's see" said Luigi. "Always use PURE PENELOPE'S SYRUP. FROOTYLICIOUS SYRUP spoils and ruins the candy." "Oh my!" screamed Luigi. That's exactly what he had done. He had strayed from the recipe and had bought FROOTYLICIOUS SYRUP because it was cheaper. Now everyone in the land was mad and the Looterelli name was ruined along with the Easter candy! The last time anyone saw Luigi, he was bouncing down the side of the mountain in a saucepan with the angry townspeople and all the Looterellis after him!

So, how important is purity? It is incredibly important! What if there were impurities in your life that spoiled your life much like the spoiled syrup ruined the Easter candy? That would be terrible, but it happens. It happens a lot. Today's scripture tells us we can keep our way pure by living according to God's Word.

How do we learn to live according to God's Word? That's a great question. We learn to live by God's Word by learning what is in God's Word. We do that by reading the Bible and by perking up our listening ears and learning at church. Asking questions of parents and teachers and memorizing Bible verses are great ways, too! God will help you remember those verses when you need them. Another way is to keep working your way through this book. There will be helpful hints all along the way. Keep plugging along.

Decide today to live the pure way and try to keep yourself from bouncing down the side of a mountain in a saucepan. We'll learn more tonight and, uh, watch out for Luigi!

Prayer: "Hiding God's Word"

*I have laid up your word in my heart
so that I will not sin against you.
Blessed are you, Oh Lord, teach me your statutes.
With my lips I recount all of the judgments of your mouth.
I rejoice in the way of your testimonies
as much as in all of the riches.
I will meditate on your precepts and
I will consider your ways.
I delight in your statutes; I will not forget your word.*
Psalm 119:11-16

O God, hiding eggs and hunting eggs at Easter are so much fun. But God, hiding your Word in my heart is so much more important. For school, I memorize math facts, spelling words and states and capitals, but if I memorize your Word, it can help me know how I should live my life. Help me learn your Word so that I don't sin against you, O God. Help me find the hidden treasure in your Word so that I live for you every day of my life.

Day 4:

"God's Strangers"

*Deal kindly with your servant and
I will live and I will keep your word.
Open my eyes that I may see the wonders of your law.
I am a stranger on earth; do not hide your
commandments from me.*
Psalm 119:17-19

Have you ever seen a picture that has images hidden within the picture? At the bottom of that picture, there are images of the items you are to find. Imagine you are looking at a picture of a jungle with trees and rocks and a river, but hidden within might be a compass, a shovel, a water canteen, a map and maybe 10 more hidden things. Very cool and so fun! You are looking at this picture and it is pretty enough by itself, but you don't realize it contains so much more.

But what if you look and look and can't find all the hidden objects? You could ask a friend to help you. What if your friend finds one or two, but that's all? What about the rest of the hidden objects?

Oh, I have an idea! Wouldn't it be great if you knew the artist who drew the picture with the hidden objects and you could ask him to help you find all of them? Yes! That would be great!

God's Word is like that. In today's scripture we read, "Open my eyes and I will see wonders of your law. . . do not hide from me your commandments." Sometimes, we can read a story from the Bible that we have read or heard many times, but this time, it seems different. We realize there is more to it than we had realized before; a new level of meaning. I wonder what amazing treasures, mysterious ways and unknown strangers God has for us to discover? Do you think God might have hidden some nuggets in there for us to find?

The psalmist knew there were wonders there in God's Word to be discovered. He prayed, "Open my eyes and I will see." Was the writer of the psalm blind? No, but he knew if he asked God to help him, God would certainly do it, because God wants us to discover all the wealth of wisdom that He put there for us to find.

Every time you open the Bible, remember that there are great things waiting for you to discover. Pray and ask God to help you find all His riches. The Bible is God's Word. He gave us His Word. Is there any reason He wouldn't want us to know all the riches He placed in His Word for us? Of course not! He's there wanting you to understand His Word and to help you through your day. Ask Him now to guide you and help you follow His ways. Then you can say with the psalmist, "I will live and I will keep your Word."

Prayer: "A Wasting Soul"

My soul wastes with longing for your judgments at all times.
Psalm 119:20

Lord, I confess I waste so many things. I waste time watching TV when Mom tells me to be doing homework. I waste too much toothpaste trying to get it on my toothbrush. I waste milk when I'm not paying attention and spill it on the table. I don't want to waste my soul. Help me to keep my mind and heart focused on you. Help me to learn about you and how you want me to live as I read from your Word each day. Help me begin to do the things I learn as I read from your Word. Give me the rest I need tonight and help me to live for you tomorrow. In Jesus' name, Amen.

Day 5:

"Arrogance"

You rebuke the arrogant who are cursed,
who stray from your commandments.
Remove from me shame and contempt,
for I have kept your testimonies.
Even though rulers sit and speak against me,
your servant will meditate on your statutes.
Psalm 119:21-23

"Oh, no!" moaned Rebecca as Dad pulled out of the church parking lot. "What's wrong?" asked Mom. "I just realized Janet was watching from the window of her grandma's apartment as I got into the car," Rebecca pouted. "What's so bad about that?" Mom wondered aloud. "Oh you just don't understand what Janet is like!" Rebecca shrieked.

Rebecca's mind was already spinning. She was thinking of when Anna came in from recess crying because of Janet making fun of her for wearing her VBS T-shirt to school. Then, she thought of Bryan crying after Janet pushed him off the playground structure while he was telling Victor about the cool illusionist who was at his church camp last summer. Then, Rebecca was thinking about when Janet and three other mean girls were making fun of Sarah for helping the little second grader who fell and skinned her knee. Yeah, Rebecca had seen Janet in action spreading around the pain when she wanted to make fun of someone or hurt them. Now, she just knew she would be on Janet's list.

Still thinking about Janet, Rebecca entered a whole new realm of stress and her stomach began to ache as she thought about her Sunday School lesson today on Jesus' words, "Blessed are you when people hate you, when they exclude you and insult you. . . Love your enemies, do good to those who hate you, bless those who curse you , pray for those who mistreat you . . . Do to others as you would have them do to you." (Luke 6:22-31) To make matters worse, she had raised her hand when Mr. Ted asked who would take the challenge to not only meditate and think on Jesus' words this week, but to really put it into practice this week and report back about it in class on Sunday. Why, oh, why had she done that? Oh wait, maybe she would have strepti-lu-mondo-chicken-itis by next Sunday. Then she wouldn't have to do any of this. Or maybe she could be chosen to go to outer space in science class tomorrow. Maybe? Even a little maybe? Yikes!

Now Rebecca has a dilemma. Will she do what Mr. Ted challenged? Will she try this week to love Janet? Will she do good to her? Will she pray for Janet?

What do you think Rebecca did? What would you have done if you had been Rebecca? What about you – do you know anyone like Janet? What did that person do to you? What would Jesus want you to do? I see. Jesus would want you to be kind to her, wouldn't He? He would want you to treat her like you want to be treated. Don't just think on these things. Go out and do them today.

Prayer: "My Delight and My Counsel"

Your testimonies are my delight, my counselors.
Psalm 119:24

Dear God, thank you for today. Help me learn to delight in your Word, your testimonies. Help me to listen to your Word and learn from it. Help me to follow what your Word teaches me like I would follow a grown-up that I know, love and trust. Your Word can give me counsel and help. Help me learn to rely on you and your Word every day of my life. In Jesus' name, Amen.

Day 6:

"Clinging to Dust"

My soul clings to the dust; give me life
according to your word.
Psalm 119:25

I love great stories. How about you? When I think of great literature, one book always leaps to the forefront of my mind – *Alexander and the Terrible, Horrible, No Good, Very Bad Day*. Poor Alexander. Everything went wrong for him. He got gum in his hair, he didn't get a window seat in the carpool, the dentist said he had a cavity, his nightlight burned out and he had to wear his railroad-train pajamas. And those were only a few of his problems! His mom said, "Some days are like that. Even in Australia."

Have you ever had a day like Alexander? I know I have. I'm guessing you have, too. How did I know that? Well, because you're human. It's part of the human experience. Our days are filled with trouble (Job 14:1). Even when we don't go looking for trouble or cause it ourselves, it seems that trouble always knows where to look for us.

What kind of troubles have you been having? Are they the general Alexander type of troubles, you know, gum in the hair, had to wear the railroad-train pajamas type of problems? Or are they something more like my best friend has started being mean to me? My parents are fighting? My dad just lost his job? My older brother's friend has been hurting me and I don't know who to tell? My grandpa is really sick and Mom doesn't think he is going to get well?

There are all kinds of problems and troubles in the world. There are so many, there's no way to list them all, but you're thinking about yours right now, aren't you? And, they cause you to hurt inside. It's normal to feel that way when you have troubles. We all feel that way when we have troubles.

The writer of this psalm knew what it meant to hurt because of his troubles. He said, "My soul clings to the dust". He was barely holding on to life! Maybe you feel that way sometimes. But don't stop there. Read on. Then he says, "Give me life according to your word." You see, the psalmist knew that God is the answer and He uses His Word to give us the answers we need for the problems in our lives. In Psalm 32:7, the writer says to God, "You are my hiding place; you will protect me from trouble and surround me with songs of deliverance." In Psalm 46:1, he says, "God is our refuge and strength, an ever present help in trouble." Our God is the God of Abraham, Isaac and Jacob. Our God is the God of Moses who dried up a path through the Red Sea and led the Children of Israel to safety. Our God is the God who helped David kill Goliath! With God as our God, no trouble is too big to face. Nothing is impossible to our God (Mark 10:27). And that's not all, in Philippians 4:13 NLT we read, "I can do everything through Christ who gives me strength." After you trust Jesus as your Savior, so can you! So there's no problem, no trouble, today that you cannot face with God's help.

Stand up with the psalmist and say, "Give me life according to your word" and with God's help go forth and face your day. Remember He is always with you. You don't have to do this alone. Let's go conquer this day, in Jesus' name! Go!

Prayer: "You Answered Me"

I have recounted my ways and you answered me;
teach me your statutes.
Psalm 119:26

God, I thank you that we can come to you in prayer. We can tell you all our hopes and dreams and fears, all our worries and troubles and problems. We can even bring our questions to you and you always answer us. That's so awesome. Grown-ups don't even answer every time. Thank you for always listening and always answering. That helps me know I'm important to you. You are important to me, too. God, please teach me your statutes – your ways. Teach me from your Word so I don't mess up my life. I want my life to be awesome and to count for you. Help me to live for you every day. In Jesus' name, Amen.

Day 7:

"Make Me"

Make me understand the way of your precepts
and I will meditate on all of your wonders.
My soul weeps from sorrow; strengthen me
according to your word.
Put away from me the way of deception;
give me life according to your law.
Psalm 119:27-29

Imagine you are lost in the jungle: you hear the heavy pounding of enormous tiger paws in full pursuit as you race recklessly through the jungle. You dodge low-hanging branches. Bushes slap you in the face. You hurdle boulders, grab vines and swing across streams. You glance back over your shoulder and see the giant cat is gaining on you with every step. As you turn to look ahead, too late, you see the pit the villagers dug to capture the man-eating tiger. There's no way to miss it. Your foot slips over the edge and you fall, for what seems like forever in slow motion – "*wwwaaaaaaaaaahhhhhhhhhhhhhhh!!!!!!!!!!*," tumbling headlong into the pit, and landing – *THWWWAAAPPP!*

Dazed, you shake your head and realize you are trapped in a deep, cold, damp, moldy pit. The stench is overwhelming. You frantically begin looking for a way out of your dilemma. *Nothing here to work with, just roots and mud* and then, in a panic, you realize there is no way out! Suddenly, you no longer smell the moldy pit. You no longer hear the jungle brush crashing under the tiger's enormous paws. You no longer hear the birds cawing or the rustle of the leaves of a million trees. Instead, deep in your bones, you feel the rumble of a blood-thirsty hot-throated growl just above your head. In extreme desperation, you begin to scream, *"hhheeeeeeeeeeeeeellllllllllllllllllllllllllllllll lllpp!!!!!!!."*

In the book of Psalms, the writer calls on God many, many times. So many times, in fact, that it shows EXTREME desperation – longing for God to help him in much the same way as we might cry out for help when the man-eating jungle tiger is about to pounce. Like the psalmist, we can be desperate for God to be at work in our lives. We can long for God to help us. We can call out to Him and run recklessly toward His commandments in much the same way as we would run recklessly away from a man-eating tiger.

Seek God by learning all you can about Him and His Word. Wake Mom and Dad on Sundays so you can be in Sunday School with your friends learning about God and what Jesus has done for you. Find out how He wants you to live. Seek out the treasures of His Word. Make your life line up with God's Word. He alone can save us from all the dangers that lurk in our daily jungles. Then you can say with the psalmist, "strengthen me . . . and . . . give me life!"

Prayer: "Running Recklessly"

I have chosen the way of faithfulness;
I have set your judgments before me.
I cling to your testimonies, Oh Lord;
do not let me be put to shame.
I run in the path of your commandments,
for you have broadened my heart.
Psalm 119:30-32

Oh God, I do choose the way of faithfulness – faithfulness to you and to your Word and your ways. I am trying to keep your judgments and your truths right before me – right in front of me – by trying to learn what you're teaching me. Help me to memorize your Word. Bring it back to my mind throughout the day. Help me to remember you wherever I am and think about things that are pleasing to you. I want to stay on the path you lay out for me. Help me not to get off track, but to walk with you every day. Thank you for a good night to rest. In Jesus' name, Amen.

Day 8:

"To the End"

Teach me, Oh Lord, the way of your statutes
and I will keep them to the end.
Give me understanding and I will keep your law
and obey it with all of my heart.
Lead me in the path of your commandments,
for in them I delight.
Psalm 119:33-35

Alex was bored. It was a warm summer morning and the day stretched endlessly before him with nothing to do – again. As he walked down the street, he noticed the giant moving van that had been in front of the large, old house at the end of the block was gone. In its place were some boxes at the curb for the garbage truck to pick up. Alex wasn't fond of garbage, but sometimes he saw interesting things that people put out as trash. It looked as if that wouldn't be the case this time–just broken plastic buckets and some dusty old books. But, oh, how Alex was wrong. Absentmindedly, Alex kicked at the box. When he did, the book on the top of the stack fell off and spilled out a single piece of paper with scraggly writing. Alex picked it up and opened the paper. What he found was amazing! It was a treasure map with riddles and clues. What could be better on a long summer day than a mystery with the hope of enormous riches at the end? He was hooked!

Alex knew his first step in solving the mystery was to get his two best friends to help. He ran home, jumped on his bike and took off to find Tiko and Mia. Once in Tiko's treehouse, Alex carefully opened the ancient–looking letter for the trio to decipher. It clearly showed the Maltese River that ran through their town. There was an 'X' in the bend of the river by a large rock formation. Tiko shrieked, "I know where that is! My family had a picnic there last summer!"

Mia was the first to leap out of the treehouse and the first on her bike as they rushed toward the river. When they got there, they found an old crate and took pieces of wood from it to dig at the base of the rock. Before long, Alex hit something. They frantically dug with their hands and soon had uncovered a glass jar with a note and a small shiny stone that shone like gold. They pored over the note and finally decided it must be leading them to the mill further up the stream at the edge of the Black Ash Forest.

They carefully followed the river's edge and began ascending the foothills of the Corona Mountain Range, at the edge of town. By mid-afternoon, the old mill was in sight. When they arrived, they compared the scene with the map and the clue. "Yep", said Mia, "this is definitely the place." Before long, they found the hollow log that the clue implied. Sure enough, there was an old burlap sack that was decaying. But inside, was a white bottle with a cork. They removed the cork and out came another clue and a small arrowhead. Gingerly, they opened the brittle paper and read the clue. They positioned the arrowhead as shown on the paper and it pointed up the mountain along the stream to a waterfall. "We must be getting close!" yelled Tiko.

They exploded up the hill at full speed. Before long they could hear the roar of the falls and it was a gorgeous sight.

But what mystery did it hold? As they approached it from the side, Mia called out over the roar, "I think I see something between the rocks behind the falls. They formed a chain and carefully Alex reached between the boulders and pulled out the weathered leather pouch. It was heavy. Their mystery was solved, but what would their treasure be?

God's Word is our treasure map. It leads us on a great quest to know Christ and join Him in His Kingdom. Within the Bible, God gives us directions and clues that help us understand and solve the great mysteries of life. Each day when we read from His Word, He gives us nuggets of truth. His commands point the way to find the riches He has prepared for us. The psalmist said, teach me your ways, and I will keep them to the end. Help me understand and I will obey with all of my heart. Each day when you open God's Word, realize that you have the most important treasure map you will ever see. It leads you straight to God's Kingdom and to His riches. Enjoy your journey with God today.

Prayer: "Turn My Eyes"

Incline my heart to your testimonies
and not to selfish gain.
Turn my eyes from seeing worthless things
and give me life in your ways.
Establish your word to your servant that
you may be feared.
Take away my disgrace which I dread,
for your judgments are good.
See how I long for your precepts;
in your righteousness give me life.
Psalm 119:36-40

Lord, I need your help with this. Help my heart and my mind to focus on you and not on worthless things. I like to win and I like to get "stuff", but help me not to be selfish. Help me to think about and focus on things that last forever, not things that break, tear up and don't really matter in the long run. Help me to get well established in your Word. Just like the roots of a tree go down deep in the ground to get the water and nutrients it needs, help my "roots" to go down deep into your Word and your ways. You are good and I want my life to count for you. In Jesus' name, Amen.

Day 9:

"Taunts"

May your steadfast love come to me, Oh Lord,
your salvation according to your word.
Then I will give an answer to the one who taunts me,
for I trust in your word.
Do not snatch the word of truth utterly from my mouth,
for I have put my hope in your judgments.
Psalm 119:41-43

Have you ever known a bully? I bet you have. You're picturing him or her right now, aren't you? Oh, I know one alright. His name is Dooley. Dooley Kanoogenflopper. (Well, that's not his real name. If I said his real name, he would come and beat me up!) Dooley was one grade ahead of me and he was about a foot taller then everyone in his grade. Dooley looked like he needed a good shave even in the 4th grade. When Dooley walked down the hall, everyone would slam themselves up against the wall, dropping their books in the process, just trying to leave Dooley plenty of room so he wouldn't give them a shove. That was just Dooley in the hallway. I don't even like to remember what he was like in the cafeteria or outside on the playground. (Ask Jason what it was like to blow mashed potatoes out of his nose or Stevey about the dandelions peeking out of his undies if you really want to know.)

I know. Your bully is just as bad. Maybe yours doesn't shove or use mashed potatoes or dandelions, but the effect is just the same. They know how to hurt you and cause you to be embarrassed and ashamed. (I wonder how they learn to do that. Maybe there's a class or workshop they attend to learn how. Maybe there's a 1-800 number to call to get tips on how to bully. Oh well, I guess some knowledge is just beyond our reach.) Sometimes, they even use their bullying to get you to do things for them that you don't want to do. Maybe they dare you. Maybe they challenge you or insult you to try to make you do the wrong things.

As terrible as that is, when it happens, (and it happens to all of us), you need to remember that 1 John 4:8 tells us that "God is love". What? Yes, remember God is love. God's kind of love is a love that makes a difference. You see, God didn't love us with just any kind of love. Jeremiah 31:3 calls it "an everlasting love". You see, God loves us so much he wanted to rescue us from the bad things of this world. He did that by sending His Son, Jesus, to die on the cross for us. After He died, God raised Him from the dead. In that way, Jesus overcame all the sin in the world. He overcame death. He overcame the grave. He overcame hell. He even overcame Dooley. And because God loves you, he can overcome your Dooley, too. You just have to trust Him as your Savior.

The writer of the psalm said, "May your steadfast love come to me, Oh Lord, your salvation according to your Word; then I will give an answer to the one who taunts me, for I trust in your Word!" God wants you to trust Him when you face your Dooleys. God is with you today. The sure-fire way to guard against the mashed potatoes and the dandelions is to walk confidently through your day, knowing

God is right there with you. When God is with you, the Dooleys aren't quite so scary. Oh yeah, by the way, God loves Dooley, too. Dooley may not know that. I wonder how Dooley could find out that God loves him? It could be that I need to tell him. Hmmm.

Prayer: "The Broad Place"

I will keep your law continually, forever and ever.
I will walk about in a broad place,
for I have sought your precepts.
Psalm 119:44-45

Dear God, thank you for your Word, your law, that teaches me how to live. As I love you and am trying to follow you, I know you will help me have a broad, smooth place for my life. I know there will be some bumpy places along the way, but you will be there with me, helping me as I continue to learn from your Word. You are awesome God! And I praise you, tonight. Help me to have sweet rest and sleep and learn more from you in the morning. In Jesus' name, Amen.

Day 10:

"Shameless"

I will speak of your testimonies before kings
and not be ashamed.
Psalm 119:46

L illy loves soccer! She thinks about her next game as soon as she opens her eyes in the morning. When she hops out of bed, her feet land on a black and white rug shaped like a soccer ball. Her favorite cereal bowl has a soccer goal on the bottom. At lunch, she talks soccer. At recess, she plays soccer. After school, she has soccer practice. When Brutus, the class bully, makes fun and tells her, "you kick like a girl," she gets right up in Brutus' face – so close she smells his stinky, boy breath and tells him, "Oh yeah? Well, I could beat you any day you're brave enough to play ball, mister!" Then she scrunches up her nose and makes her, "I mean business" game day face. With her hands on her hips, she stares down Brutus and he walks away muttering to himself.

On Sunday, Lilly goes to church with her family. Lilly is a Christian. Lilly's Sunday School teacher, Mrs. Kate, challenged everyone in class to tell three people what they

learned in church on Sunday and to invite those three kids to church next week.

Throughout the week, Lilly thought about Mrs. Kate's challenge. Lilly thought about all her friends at school and tried to imagine telling them about God and her Sunday School lesson. Each time she thought about inviting them to church, it felt like two million butterflies in her stomach. Sadly, each day the opportunity would pass and Lilly would feel guilty. Lilly could talk with anyone about soccer. Why was it so hard to talk with them about God?

How much of Lilly's day involved soccer? Hmmm. It seems like she had soccer on her mind most of the day. She thought about it, talked about it, practiced it and played it. When challenged, she could stand up and defend it. She practically oozed soccer.

When we spend time with God and His word, it is natural for that to come out of us. When we know great things about God, we will want to share those great things with others. When we're thinking about God, it is natural to talk about Him to others. When you squeeze an orange, what comes out? Orange juice. It's natural. Let's spend time with God and His Word, talk with God, and learn about Him from His Word. When we fill our day with God and His Word, He's bound to come out. It's only natural.

Prayer: "Raised Hands"

I delight in your commandments because I love them.
I lift up my hands unto your commandments which I love
and I meditate on your statutes.
Psalm 119:47-48

Lord, just like Lilly from this morning, I love soccer (or baseball, or dance, or football, or _____) and I get so excited at those games. I yell and cheer and clap and throw up my hands. I get so excited about the things I love. Help me to get so excited about you and your Word that I raise my hands to you in reverence and praise. Help me to remember what I read and think on it through the day. Help me to learn your Word and memorize it so that I can take it with me wherever I go. I love you, Lord. In Jesus' name, Amen.

Day 11:

"My Comfort"

Remember the word to your servant,
for I have put my hope in it.
This is my comfort in my affliction,
that your word gives me life.
The arrogant mock me exceedingly,
but I have not turned from your law.
I remember your judgments from of old, Oh Lord,
and I am comforted by them.
Psalm 119:49-52

Sssnnnnnn, sssnnniifffff? Uuuuummmmmm, popcorn. With butter, *mmmmmm*. I love that smell. Or, how about when you walk in the back door and immediately you smell Mama's warm, ooey-gooey chocolate chip cookies fresh from the oven. *Yuummmm!* Happy smells.

Think back to when you were a little kid. Did you have a favorite blanket? Maybe you had a teddy bear that went everywhere with you. Did it help you feel secure? Something familiar you could snuggle close? It just felt right. It smelled right. It was just what you needed and it was very comforting.

Do you remember Charlie Brown and Snoopy? How about Linus and his blanket? The blanket was with Linus wherever he went. When Linus had a problem, the blanket was always a part of the solution. The blanket was very important and it was always there with Linus.

When we're little kids, blankets are okay for comfort. But what about now? How would you feel carrying your baby blanket to sixth grade math? NO WAY! So where's our comfort for today? Huh?

God's Word reminds me a little bit of Linus' blanket. God's Word is able to comfort us when we need it. When we learn God's Word and memorize it, it is always with us. Always. We take it with us, in our mind, everywhere we go. So God's Word can go with us to math class, on the volleyball court, on the soccer field, in the gym locker room – everywhere.

When you have problems, God's Word is there. When you have troubles, God's Word is there. When you're scared, God's Word can help you not be afraid. When you can't sleep, God's Word can help you "lie down and sleep in peace, for you alone, O LORD, make me dwell in safety" (Psalm 4:8) and that God who watches over you, "will not sleep or slumber" (Psalm 121:4). When you're confused, God's Word helps make things clear. When you don't know what you should do, God's Word can give you direction.

The Bible says, God's Word will last forever. That means when you're a kid and even when you're old, God's Word will still be there to bring you comfort. Favorite blankets and chocolate chip cookies come and go, but God's Word is with us forever. Oh, what comfort.

Prayer: "My Song"

Rage seizes me because of the wicked
who have forsaken your law.
Your statutes have been my song
in the house of my journey.
I remember in the night your name, Oh Lord,
and I will keep your law.
This is my practice: I keep your precepts.
Psalm 119:53-56

Lord, as I go through my day and look around me, I see many who do not follow you or your laws. I see people doing many bad things. I thank you and praise you that you are teaching me to follow your ways. As I think about you tonight while I get ready for bed, I remember all the good things you have taught me. You have taught me to be kind and caring toward others, to help them and to tell them about you. I want that to be my way of life. I want to live a life that pleases you. Help me to be this way every day. Let my life be like a song of praise to you as I try to do what you want me to. And help me remember to sing songs of praise to you every day. In Jesus' name, Amen.

Day 12:

"My Portion"

*The Lord is my portion; I have promised
to keep your word.
I have sought your face with my whole heart;
give me life according to your word.
I have considered my ways and I have turned
my feet unto your testimonies.*
Psalm 119:57-59

"**M**OM! DeShaun took my part of the funnel cake! I had the big half and he grabbed it and took off!"

"Deja, stop whining. You've had a lot and there's plenty more," Mom called over her shoulder as she turned to the right beside the giant gopher statue.

Deja wouldn't stop. She stomped her foot, closed her eyes, screamed and refused to go one step more. She was mad and wanted what was hers. It had been a long, tiring day at the amusement park and it had drained every last ounce of patience from her. She wanted what was hers and she wasn't budging from her spot until she got it!

She expected to feel Mom's hand on her shoulder. She expected DeShaun to say, "Oh, okay Deja. Here's your piece." But she didn't feel Mom's hand and she didn't hear DeShaun's voice. She opened one eye, not wanting them to see she was looking, but with that one eye, she didn't see anyone that she knew. When she opened both eyes, Mom,

Dad, DeAndre and DeShaun were nowhere in sight. She looked all around her to see if they were hiding, but she didn't see them anywhere. She called their names, but they didn't answer. This didn't seem right. Mom would never leave her alone in a place like this even if it was to teach her a lesson. Deja knew something was wrong. She was scared and she took off to find them. She took off running. She ran past the giant gopher and straight up the hill – farther away from her family with every step. Everywhere she looked, she saw strangers. Nothing looked familiar. The amusement park that was usually a fun place had quickly turned into a scary place. Deja strained her eyes for a glimpse of Mom's face, but there was no one who looked familiar. This time when Deja began to cry, it wasn't for her portion of the funnel cake. It was for real.

An hour later, when Mom turned the corner into the security guard's office, it was the sweetest face Deja had ever seen. Mom had been frantically searching for her the entire time. Now that they were back together, Deja was never going to let her out of her sight.

Today's scripture tells us, "The Lord is my portion . . . I have sought your face with my whole heart". The Lord can be your portion. He is the best part of everything. When you seek Him with your whole heart, you will find Him (Jeremiah 29:13). He has been seeking you for your entire life. Open up your eyes. Spend time with Him in His Word. He is your portion.

Prayer: "Quickly"

I will hasten and not delay to keep your commandments.
Psalm 119:60

Lord, here we are back to this "hurry up and not delay to mind you". I have trouble with this sometimes. I want to do right. I want to obey Mom and Dad right away, but sometimes I forget. Sometimes I get distracted. Sometimes I just decide not to obey. I know that's wrong. Please forgive me and help me to do right. Sometimes I have trouble doing that with what you teach me, too. Sometimes I know what I should do and I just choose not to do it. I'm sorry, God. Please forgive me. Please help me to grow to where I want to mind you all the time. As soon as I realize you're nudging me to do something, please help me to hurry up and not delay to obey. I know that will please you. That's what I want to do. Please help me, God. In Jesus' name, Amen.

Day 13:

"Midnight"

The cords of the wicked have bound me;
I have not forgotten your law.
In the middle of the night, I rise to thank you
for your righteous judgments.
Psalm 119:61-62

Marco could hear them going at it again. It started right after he went to bed. He tried to go to sleep so he wouldn't hear it, but every night it was the same. Dad would yell. Mom would cry. Only, tonight it was worse. He heard a kitchen chair fall over and he heard some glass breaking. Then, he heard the front door open and slam shut.

Now the car is driving away and Mom is crying. What if Dad doesn't come back?

Maybe this has happened in your home. Maybe not. If not, you are very fortunate and blessed. Maybe something has happened and it's not exactly the same, but still you lie there and think about it in your bed. You want to go to sleep so you don't have to remember it, but sleep stays away to leave you lying there in your bed afraid and wondering about the future.

Friend, you are not alone. Many people have troubles that keep them awake in the middle of the night. Even if parents aren't arguing and fighting, other problems come to mind when we get still and aren't distracted by things like homework, video games and favorite television shows. When it's still and quiet, conversations replay and images begin to flash across the giant screen in our minds, showing us, in vivid details, things that we would sometimes rather forget. Even the fellow who wrote this psalm was facing an intense situation with evil people. He was so troubled, he was awake in the middle of the night like you. When troubles and problems come to mind, it is natural for us to respond with panic or anger, or to create a plan to get even with those who are hurting us. But that's not what this psalmist did. He began to praise God and thank Him for His Word. Say what!?!? That's right. He praised God for His awesome Word.

You see, in God's Word, we find many, many things. We find comfort when we're scared and hurting. We find answers for our troubles. We find encouragement when we are struggling. We find help when we are helpless.

We learn from God's Word that you can give all your worries and cares to God because He cares for you (1 Peter 5:7). We learn that the name of the LORD is a strong tower – a safe haven – we can run to and be safe (Proverbs 18:10). We learn that some put their trust in physical things, but we can trust in the strong name of the LORD our God (Psalm 20:7). We learn that the LORD your God is with you. He is mighty enough to save. He adores you and He will quiet you with his love. God, Himself, will rejoice over you with singing (Zephaniah 3:17). And we learn that you can lie down and sleep in peace, for only God can keep you safe (Psalm 4:8) and He is always awake and always watching over you to keep you safe and steady (Psalm 121:3-4).

So when you wake in the night or have trouble going to sleep, turn your mind to God and His Word. Thank Him that He is with you and will help you through this day. And remember all His promises to help you and keep you. Cares and worries? Give them to God and forget them. Get on with your day and praise the Lord!

Prayer: "Friends"

I am a companion to all who fear you,
to those who keep your precepts.
Your steadfast love fills the earth; teach me your statutes.
Psalm 119:63-64

Lord, thank you for my friends. Even with all the friends I have, I know I have a choice of who to hang around with. Help me choose my friends wisely. Help me to have good friends who love you and who follow your ways. Help me to be that kind of friend, too. Even with those people I know who don't follow you, help me to be a good example for them to follow. Help them to see me following you. Let my life be a shining example, like a light, they can follow that helps them come to you. Thank you for your enormous love that took your Son, Jesus, to the cross for my sins. Thank you for loving me that much. Help me live for you. In Jesus' name, Amen.

Day 14:

"Affliction"

You have done good with your servant,
according to your word, Oh Lord.
Teach me knowledge and good judgment,
for I believe in your commandments.
Before I was afflicted I strayed, but now I keep your word.
You are good and do good; teach me your statutes.
The arrogant have forged lies against me, but I will keep
your precepts with all of my heart.
Their heart is unfeeling as fat, but I delight in your law.
It was good for me that I was afflicted so that
I might learn your statutes.
Psalm 119:65-71

The dark clouds behind the raindrops pelting the window of Ivan's hospital room matched the mood in his room. The rumbling thunder underscored the doctor's grim words, "the tests show that Ivan has cancer." Mom began to cry. Dad asked a million questions. The doctor answered many of those by saying, "I don't know. We will have to do more tests."

Ivan's mind swirled. How could a nine-year old kid have cancer? Isn't that supposed to happen to old people? How many more tests can there be? He had already been in the hospital nine days. They had pretty much been doing tests on him all day, every day.

When he wasn't having a test, they let him go to the playroom. He liked that room. It was bright and cheerful. It had toys and games, a huge salt-water aquarium with beautiful neon-bright fish. A train ran around the room on a track above the windows and doors.

It was here that he met Nora and Chance. Both of them were in wheelchairs. Both of them had cancer. Neither of them had any hair. Chance had been there the longest. He had been there for four months. Nora had only been there five weeks. Ivan liked Chance the best. Chance liked to talk with Ivan. Chance smiled, too. When Ivan wasn't feeling very well, Chance would say things like, "Hang on. It will get better." Or, "It won't hurt all the time. If I can do this, you can, too!"

Nora wasn't like that, though. She scowled a lot. When the three of them tried to play a game, Nora would get angry every time. Once, she grabbed the game board and threw it into the floor. Sometimes, she would cry and scream and hit things, too.

Chance told Ivan he had felt the way Nora does, at times, but deep down he knows God is with him, helping him go through this difficult time. Now that Ivan has heard the words, "Ivan has cancer," he wonders if he will choose to be more like Chance or more like Nora.

Even when our difficulties, our afflictions, aren't as serious or as life-threatening as cancer, we still have a choice of how to respond to our circumstances. For example, if there were problems in your family, would you be angry at God or would you thank Him for helping you through the difficulties each day? What if you had more difficulty learning than some others in your class seem to have? Would you be angry and say, "It's not worth it, I quit!" or would you thank God that you get to go to school to read and learn? And – would you trust Him to help you even though it's hard?

Every day, we choose how we are going to face our difficulties. Today, with Jesus as our helper, let's choose to say with the psalmist, Lord, "you have done good for your servant. . . Teach me. . . It was good for me that I was afflicted so that I might learn your statutes."

Prayer: "Better than Gold"

The law from your mouth is better to me than thousands of pieces of gold and silver.
Psalm 119:72

Lord, you know I love stuff. Toys, games, clothes, money, all kinds of stuff. In my head, I know you and your Word are better than all the stuff in the world. But sometimes, it's hard to remember that when I'm around my friends and they start talking about all their "stuff". Help me to get to know your Word and fall in love with your Word so much that all the "stuff" doesn't seem as important. Teach me. Please be patient with me and help me learn to value the things of God more than all the stuff. In Jesus' name, Amen.

Day 15:

"His Hands"

Your hands made me and formed me;
give me understanding and I will learn your
commandments.
Psalm 119:73

"Kendrick!" called Dad from the kitchen, "it's time to read your Bible and then get ready for bed." Kendrick whined, "Aww Dad, what's the use? I never understand what it means!" Dad put down the dish he was putting away and came into the den and sat down by Kendrick. "It's frustrating and no fun when you don't understand, isn't it?" asked Dad. "Yes," replied Kendrick. Dad said, "Well, let's think about this for a minute. Do you remember when Grandma gave you that model airplane for your birthday and you tried putting it together without reading the instructions? It was difficult and not very fun, right?" Kendrick nodded his head. Dad continued, "But when you sat down and followed the pictures in the instructions, think how much easier it became." "I know the model plane was easier when I used the pictures," pouted Kendrick, "but there aren't pictures in my Bible for every verse." "That's true," agreed Dad, "but think about this – you know the Author of the Book." "What?" asked Kendrick as he perked up. "Even better than that, you know the One who breathed life into His book," Dad countered.

"What do you mean?" Kendrick followed. Dad continued, "Tell me your memory verse from Sunday School last week." Kendrick quoted, "All Scripture is God-breathed and is useful for teaching, rebuking, correcting and training in righteousness 2 Timothy 3:16." "That's right," added Dad, "so God breathed life into Scripture. Now let's look up Genesis 2:7 which says, *God formed the man from the dust of the ground and breathed into his nostrils the breath of life, and the man became a living being.*" "That was Adam," announced Kendrick. "You're right!" said Dad, "and it gets even better." Kendrick was hooked now. Dad continued, "From Psalm 139, we know that God created you! So don't you think the God who breathed life into His Word and who breathed life into Adam and breathed life into you can help you understand what His Word is saying to you? We just need to ask him for His help!" "OK," said Kendrick.

Dad and Kendrick knelt down by the sofa and bowed their heads, Kendrick prayed, "God I'm having trouble understanding what I'm reading down here. Will you help me? I want to understand what you want to teach me from your instruction Book, but the words are big and hard. Help me to see and understand the part I need to understand right now and help me keep learning and growing my whole life to be the person you want me to be. I think it's really cool how You breathed life into your Word and you breathed life into me. Help me remember that all day today. In Jesus' name, Amen."

Prayer: "A Beautiful Sight"

*May those who fear you see me and rejoice because I
have put my hope in your word.*
Psalm 119:74

*Lord, thank you for my church friends. It's good to have
friends who know you and love you and believe the same
things I do. Lord, please help me to live my life so that it
encourages them. Help me to live in such a way that I can
be an example to them. When they are discouraged, let
them be encouraged by watching me follow you. May they
be strengthened to try again to do what is right. When they
are sad, help me to help lift them up. When they don't know
what to do, help me lead them to seek you and follow you.
It is good to be a part of the family of God and to be with
my Christian brothers and sisters. Make me a blessing to
them. Thank you, God, for being so good to me. I love you.
In Jesus' name, Amen.*

Day 16:

"Love"

I know, Oh Lord, that your judgments are righteous,
and in faithfulness you have afflicted me.
May your steadfast love comfort me, according
to your word to your servant.
May your compassion come to me and I will live,
for your law is my delight.
Psalm 119:75-77

Rosa's life was filled with trouble. She had nowhere to turn, no one to turn to. She felt very alone. Rosa's mom had gotten married six months ago. At first, Rosa was hoping everything would get better, that they would have more money – enough to pay their bills and buy food, hoping that Mom would not be stressed anymore and they could do things as a family. But now she realized, those were all just dreams and none of them had come true.

Rosa's stepdad drank. As a matter of fact, he stayed drunk most of the time. And when he was drunk, he was mean. So nothing was better – everything was worse. They didn't have *more* money. They had less because her stepdad couldn't keep a job because he was drunk most of the time. The money her mom made at the factory still wasn't enough. Her mom tried to hide the money for their food, but Rosa's stepdad usually found it and would take it to go buy more beer. They almost never had anything to eat for breakfast or dinner. The only meal Rosa got was lunch at school.

Early one Sunday morning while Rosa and her mom were sleeping, Rosa's stepdad came in from drinking all night. He was yelling and cursing and turning over the furniture and throwing things. Rosa and her mom climbed out a window of the bedroom and ran toward the street. As they rounded a corner, they ran into their neighbor, Mrs. Sanchez. Mrs. Sanchez knew they were frightened and Mom was crying. Mrs. Sanchez was always nice to them. She took them into her apartment, got them something to eat and told them she was going to church and invited them to go with her. Mom didn't want to go, but they had nowhere to stay so she finally agreed. Mrs. Sanchez said Mom could go to her ladies class, and Rosa could go to the children's class. When Rosa was introduced to her teachers, they were very kind to her. They invited her over to a circle of chairs where they were about to tell a story from the Bible. Rosa had heard of the Bible but didn't know any of the stories.

Rosa learned about three Hebrew children who had troubles of their own. They had been kidnapped by an invading army and taken away from their families to be slaves in a foreign land. Later, when they refused to obey evil men, they were thrown into the fire to be killed. But something amazing happened. They didn't die, but just walked around in the fire! The king called the three Hebrews out of the fire. They walked out and their clothes weren't burned and they didn't even smell like smoke. The teacher said, "God took care of them and if He can take care of them, He can take care of you, too."

Rosa felt much better after that. She liked knowing that God loved her and that he would be with her no matter what. Mom liked Mrs. Sanchez's church. They decided they would go back next week and learn some more about God and the Bible.

Rosa learned something that day that we should always remember – God's steady, never-ending love is comforting. He never leaves us, never forsakes us. He has compassion for us. That means He is very caring and kind, like Rosa's teachers. After we trust Jesus as our Savior, He will always be with us no matter what we face. No matter what we go through, He will be right there with us. Even if our circumstances don't change, knowing that God is with us and is there to help us through whatever we face is enough. Let's remember that today. And remember how Mrs. Sanchez invited her friends (Rosa and her mom) who were having such a rough time to go to church with her? Keep your eyes and ears open today. Is there someone you know that you need to invite to church with you? That may be exactly what God wants you to do today.

Prayer: "Falsely Accused"

*May the arrogant be ashamed for they
have wronged me falsely;
I will meditate on your precepts.
May those who fear you turn to me,
those who know your testimonies.
May my heart be blameless in your statutes
so that I will not be ashamed.*
Psalm 119:78-80

God, thank you for this day. Lord, some days are harder than other days. Sometimes, mean people say things about me that aren't true. Please help me live my life in a way so that others will know that I don't do those bad things others' claimed I did. Help me to think about and learn your Word so much that it makes a difference in my everyday life. Help me to live so that I please you every day. In Jesus' name, Amen.

Day 17:

"Gloriously Faint"

My soul languishes for your salvation;
I hope in your word.
My eyes fail for your words, saying
"when will you comfort me?"
Psalm 119:81-82

"Mom, I think you better come in here," called Jean-Luc.

"What is it?" asked Mom as she entered the darkened room and turned on the lamp. Jean-Luc continued, "I think something's wrong. I'm seeing spots!"

Marcel giggled, "It's because he's been staring at the computer game screen through 19 levels of Savatron and when he got stuck on level 16, I had to show him how to find the cheat codes online to go to the next level when he was stuck in the outer mud rim on planet Mulgari."

"Sounds like that's enough Savatron for tonight" said Mom as she took the computer game and replaced it with his Bible. "Tonight's Scripture passage is Psalm 119:81-82. Read that for Marcel and me, please."

Jean-Luc read, "My soul languishes for your salvation, I have put my hope in your Word. My eyes fail for your Words, saying when will you comfort me?"

"What does 'languish' mean?" asked Marcel.

"Do you see that Christmas Poinsettia over there on the table that Aunt Colette sent for Christmas?" asked Mom.

"You mean the dead Christmas flower in the corner?" inquired Jean-Luc.

"That's the one" replied Mom. "It languished for water until it died." Mom said.

"Oh, sorry about that," Marcel said with a goofy look on his face, "I forgot to water it a time or two when you reminded me."

"Uh huh" said Mom.

"What does the rest of this mean?" asked Jean-Luc trying to get Marcel out of the hot seat.

"Well," said Mom sitting down on the footstool, "the writer of this Psalm had searched the Scriptures to find a way to make it through life when he was stuck in a difficult place – much like you when you were stuck in the outer mud rim on the planet Mudpuddle."

"Mulgari!" shouted the boys.

"So what did you do when you couldn't get unstuck?" asked Mom.

"Marcel showed me how to find my way through the hard part with the cheat codes!" exclaimed Jean-Luc.

"That's right," said Mom. "But the psalmist wasn't looking for a cheat code. He was just looking to God's instruction Book to find how to get through the rough part of life. And unlike *you*, who stared at the computer game until you saw spots, the psalmist was reading page after page after page of God's Word, digging deeper and deeper trying to find the answers until his eyes were so blurry it was hard to see!"

"Wow!" mused Jean-Luc, "I have never read that many words in my whole life."

"Well maybe you should try that next time instead of playing 19 levels of Savage Train," called Mom over her shoulder as she left the room.

"Savatron!" the boys shouted in unison.

"And now I'm going to finish making dinner so you boys don't languish for food like Aunt Colette's gift languished for water," Mom called.

Marcel giggled and Jean-Luc followed him into the kitchen. Jean-Luc exclaimed, "I'm sure glad Mom knows the cure for languishing. I'm starved!"

Prayer: "In the Smoke"

For I have been like a wineskin in the smoke;
I have not forgotten your statutes.
Psalm 119:83

Dear God, some days are hard. Sometimes I feel like the heat is really on and everything I try goes wrong. Sometimes I feel like everyone is against me. Sometimes, I don't even feel like opening the Bible to read what you say. I am tempted to just stay in my misery and whine and wallow in it. Lord, even on difficult days, help me look to your Word for the help and encouragement I need to make it. Help me grow to where my first thought is always to turn to you. I love you, God. Thank you for always being there and listening to me and answering my prayers. In Jesus' name, Amen.

Day 18:

"Facing Death"

How long are the days of your servant?
When will you execute judgment on those
who persecute me?
The arrogant dig pits for me,
which are not in keeping with your law.
All of your commandments are faithful;
they persecute me falsely – help me.
They almost destroyed me on the earth,
but I have not forsaken your precepts.
Psalm 119:84-87

Bristol was tired and scared. Tired of the way she was treated all the time at school. Scared because the threats and taunts continued to get meaner. She always had a knot in her stomach at school, afraid of what was around the next corner or at lunch or in the gym. Being at home wasn't much better. It was hard to concentrate on homework. It only made her think of "them". When she went to bed, they were there in her thoughts.

Mom tried to listen and understand, but she really didn't get it. She would tell her things to do or say, but those didn't work. Mom talked to the teacher. Mrs. Styles was nice to her, but the mean kids didn't do things where she could see. They always waited until no adult could see. That's what made it so bad. Some of the teachers even *thought* these kids were good kids. At least, they were good at pretending.

Bristol didn't really even know why they didn't like her. She had tried to be nice to them. She even tried to tell them about Jesus once and that only seemed to make it worse. It was like once they knew she was a Christian, they turned up the heat.

Bristol hadn't even dared to breathe this to anyone, but sometimes she even wondered if she would live through this. "How could this be happening to me? How could there be so many mean people? Why would they pick on me? Why would they tell such lies?" Bristol wondered. She felt like today's verse says, "They almost destroyed me."

Most days she just went through the motions, doing what she had to do. Some Sundays, she and Mom would go to church. It was okay, but no one there really knew what was going on in her life. None of them were facing what she was facing; at least that was what she thought until this week. This Sunday, her teachers, Mr. and Mrs. Bartley were telling about Christians around the World who endured threats and mistreatment. They even talked about something called the Persecuted Church. Bristol found out some people were lied about, beaten, put in prison and even killed because of their faith. She never knew that. Why would people be so mean? But then, Mr. Bartley read them Isaiah 51:7-8 NIrV, "Listen to me, you who know what is right. Pay attention, you who have my law in your hearts. Do not be afraid when mere people make fun of you. Do not be terrified when they laugh at you. They will be like clothes that moths have eaten up. They will be like wool that worms have chewed up. But my saving power will last forever. I will save you for all time to come."

Bristol was so excited to hear this. God knew what was going on in her life and His saving power will last forever. As today's verse says, God's commandments are faithful and he is able to help her. Now she knew she needed to pray for these mean kids for God to change their lives. Bristol had a new mission now, to be an ambassador for Christ to the kids at school (2 Corinthians 5:20). Now her life had meaning and purpose and she had a way to go on, walking daily with Jesus at her side.

Prayer: "Live to Obey"

According to your steadfast love, give me life and I will keep the testimonies of your mouth.
Psalm 119:88

Lord, thank you for your love. You show your love to me in so many ways – my family; my church; giving your Son, Jesus; listening to my prayers; caring for me; forgiving me. Your Word tells me that you are love (1 John 4:8) and that your perfect love drives out our fear (1 John 4:18). Thank you that I don't have to be afraid. Help me live every day in a way that shows I love you and follow you. In Jesus' name, Amen.

Day 19:

"Stationed in the Heavens"

Forever, Oh Lord, your word is stationed in the heavens.
Your faithfulness continues
from generation to generation;
you established the earth and it stands firm.
Your judgments stand today,
for all of them are your servants.
Psalm 119:89-91

"Oh, Dad, when I was working on my homework on your computer, it said you need to update your operating system before I can finish my science project on the constellations. Would you pass the green beans, please?" "Here you go, Sheridan," said Mom. "And Mom?" said Jessie. "Yes Jessie?" "I need help downloading the updates on my iTunes account. I tried, but something didn't work right." "Okay dear, I'll help you after dinner," agreed Mom. "Dad?" questioned Anthony. "What is it, Anthony?" answered Dad. Anthony explained, "My teacher says I have to edit and rewrite my paragraph about my favorite cartoon character! What's wrong with Scooby Doo anyway? How can I make it any better? Scooby's the greatest! Why do I have to change it?"

"Whoa, whoa slow down," said Dad. "You're all just running into some of the things we face in this world – constant change. Did you read your devotion this morning?

Remember what it said?" "I remember it was something about the heavens because it reminded me I hadn't finished my project about the constellations." said Sheridan. "That's right," said Dad. "I've got it right here. *Forever, Oh Lord, your Word has been stationed in the heavens.*" "Oh yeah," chimed Jessie, "I didn't understand all of that." "Well," Dad continued, "God's Word never changes because it reflects God's nature. And, what is one thing we know about God?" "That He's very old!" added Anthony. "You're close, Anthony. We see from Hebrews 13:8 that He is the same yesterday, today and forever! God never changes and His Word never changes," Dad said. "You mean there are no updates or upgrades?" quipped Jessie with a smile. "That's exactly what it means," smiled Dad. "And Sheridan, speaking of the constellations, the book of Amos in the Old Testament mentions Orion and the Pleiades constellations. The book of Job mentions both of these and the Bear constellation." "Those are in my science project! You mean they're in the Bible, too?" asked Sheridan. Dad laughed, "Yes, I saw them on the screen while you were working earlier. And yes, they're in the Bible! Who do you think created all those constellations you're studying in science?" "Well, God did," said Sheridan. "Exactly," said Dad, "Now you're beginning to see how God's Word, which is stationed in the heavens, never changes from generation to generation. That's how we can base our life on it. It was true when I was 12 and it is still true now that I am 20." "You're 47!" laughed Jessie. "Yes," laughed Dad, "and it was true when my great, great granddad preached from it and it will be true when Anthony here is an old, old man with grandkids watching Scooby Doo's great grand puppies on their cartoons." Everybody laughed and Mom said,

"The Bible teaches us about God and how to serve Him. It helps us become more like Jesus every day. That's why we read it, study it and try to live by it. Now, who's ready for dessert?" "Me!" "I am!" "Ooh me!" "Bring on the Yummy!"

Prayer: "If Not"

If your law had not been my delight, then I would have perished in my affliction.
Psalm 119:92

Wow, God. Thank you for today. There were some really good things today, like _____ (name some of those things). There were some hard things today, too, like _____ (name some of those things). Thank you for being with me through all the ups and downs of every day. It's great to have you with me in the good times, but I wouldn't make it if you weren't with me during the hard times. I need your help and your strength in my life. I'm going to hold on to you so tightly that nothing could pry me away from you. Thank you, God, for holding on to me and never letting me go (Romans 8:39). I trust in you, O God my Strength (Psalm 59:17).

Day 20:

"I Am Yours"

Forever, I will not forget your precepts,
for by them you have given me life.
I am yours; save me, for I have sought your precepts.
The wicked wait to destroy me;
I will consider your testimonies.
Psalm 119:93-95

Emmaline followed along after her mother, nibbling grass along the way. It was a warm sunny day in the meadow. These were her favorite kind of days, playing with her friends and staying close to Mom. "Something is happening over at the other side of the sheep pen," Emmaline thought to herself. Everyone was running toward her. She couldn't figure out what was going on. Then she heard it – a voice she had never heard before – a stranger's voice. There were men she had never seen before. They were chasing and grabbing sheep from her flock. Emmaline was scared and ran as fast as she could, trying to stay right beside her mother. But wait, now she hears the familiar voice of her shepherd. He chased the robbers away and then came and began to speak softly to the sheep in his flock. He told them it was okay now and he was there to take care of them. The restless sheep began to settle down. Some looked around nervously, but others began to nibble at the grass in the meadow. Some of the older sheep began to lie down near the shepherd. Emmaline's mom decided it was okay to lie down. Emmaline was glad. Being afraid and running so fast had made her very tired. She was so glad she had a good shepherd to take care of her.

In John 10:27, we read where Jesus says, "My sheep listen to my voice; I know them, and they follow me." For those who have trusted in Jesus as Savior, we belong to Jesus; we are in His flock. "We are his people, the sheep of His pasture" (Psalm 100:3b), and no one can take us away from Him. He's got his sheep and He's holding on to them.

In the story above, Emmaline and the sheep in her flock knew their shepherd's voice. But how would we get to know Jesus' voice? We get to know His voice by spending time in His Word, the Bible. God's Word always points to Jesus – always tells us more about Him. As we spend time with Him, reading in His Word, we get to know Him. We learn His voice. When there are threats from the world, and we are hearing strange voices we don't know trying to pull us away, we will know they are not from our flock. We will know they are not from our Shepherd. We will know they are not safe to trust – not safe to follow. Jesus is our Good Shepherd. Today, I will follow Him and remember His precepts – His Word. How about you?

Prayer: "Limitless"

To all perfection I have seen an end,
but your commandments are exceedingly broad.
Psalm 119:96

Hi Lord. Thank you for this day. Thank you for being with me today and helping me. Lord, I have seen some things that aren't perfect. I've taken a few tests at school that didn't turn out perfect. I missed some problems on my math homework the other day. I'm not very good at perfection. You know that already. I know I will never be perfect, but with your help, I'm growing to be more like you. But, Lord, I know your Word is perfect. It is exactly right. It is never wrong – never partially wrong – always bullseye perfect. I can count on you and your Word to always be the same, to never change. You are the same yesterday, today and forever (Hebrews 13:8). I'm so glad I can always count on you. Good night, Lord. I'll talk with you tomorrow. In Jesus' name, Amen.

Day 21:

"Surpassing Wisdom"

Oh how I love your law! I meditate on it all of the day.
Your commandments make me wiser than my enemies, for
they are forever with me.
I have more insight than all my teachers,
for I meditate on your statutes.
I have more understanding than the elders,
because I have kept your precepts.
Psalm 119:97-100

Sanjay was the smartest kid in class. He always had been – every year the same – except this year. This year a new girl had moved into town. Her name was Eva.

Eva was a little bit different. She read her Bible at lunch. She brought cards with Bible verses on them. She worked at memorizing them. Some days at recess, she would stop, pull a card out of her pocket, re-read it and then she would go on climbing back up on the jungle gym.

Sanjay still knew lots of stuff – science facts, multiplication tables, you know, school stuff. But when Mrs. Nguyen asked questions that weren't just about facts to recite – you know, the questions where you have to think and figure out the answers, Eva beat Sanjay every time. Mrs. Nguyen said Eva is wise.

What do you suppose made Eva wise? You're right! Learning and meditating on God's Word. The Bible tells us that over and over. I wonder why that's so hard to remember? The thing is that learning Bible facts is important – very important. But the Bible tells us in James 1:22, that we should not only listen to what the Bible says, we should do what it says. We should learn it and then do it.

Being wise helps us in our daily lives. People who are wise are able to navigate around some problems in life that people who are unwise wind up stuck in. People who are unwise usually have very difficult lives because they make a lot of bad choices with lots of bad consequences.

How would you like to be wise? Are you doing all the things you have already learned from the Bible? We should try to do those things we have learned from God's Word every day. Some days we get it right and some days we get it wrong, but the important thing is to keep working at it every day. God loves you and wants to help you. Learning from the Bible is what makes you wise for salvation through faith in Christ Jesus (2 Timothy 3:15). So let's do this together today. We're starting our day on the right foot. We have learned from God's Word and now we're off to do what it says. Go Team!

Prayer: "My Teacher"

I have withheld my feet from every evil path
so that I might keep your word.
I have not turned away from your judgments,
for you have taught me.
Psalm 119:101-102

God, thank you for today. It's been a good day, well, a pretty good day. I've tried really hard to do what's right, to stay on your path and not get on the wrong path. I have tried to keep your Word today. I have tried to remember the things you're teaching me. I didn't get it all exactly right, but I'm learning and I'm trying. Thank you for helping me. I love you, Lord. Please help me to sleep well tonight and to walk with you tomorrow. In Jesus' name, Amen.

Day 22:

"Like Honey"

How sweet are your words to my taste,
more than honey to my mouth.
Psalm 119:103

Zach, Jacob and Darnell always turned left onto Maple Street as they walked home from school. It would have been faster to pass Maple Street, turn left onto Oak Street and then climb through the fence to get to their apartment building, but if they did that, they wouldn't walk past the Maple Street Bakery and they wouldn't see Ms. Shelly.

Ms. Shelly was a round, little lady with frizzy red hair peeking out from her hair net and flour on her face. Ms. Shelly was nice and always laughing and smiling. And, oh, the sweetest smells were always drifting out of the bakery and hovering over the sidewalk – strawberry, lemon, chocolate, butter and honey! Somehow, those smells caused our feet to follow our noses right into her bakery. Every afternoon, she would have three glasses of milk and three of her "disaster" cookies or some "oopsy daisy" muffins – yummy surprises tucked away for us – you know, the ones she thought didn't look "just right". But, oh, they tasted "just right." Every afternoon was a feast of the finest treats.

Today's verse says God's words are sweeter than honey. Well, what does that mean? Is it like a scratch and sniff thing? No, it's talking about something entirely different. It

means when we start really paying attention to what we're reading, when we make it a part of our lives to spend time in God's Word every day, it will become something we long for. The more we spend time with God, the more we will want to spend with Him. We will be learning so much, practicing so much of what we're learning, and God will be helping us in ways we never knew possible. It will be so awesome – like the greatest tasting treat in the world!

What's that? You say when you read, it's not quite like that. Right? Well, that's right. But that's why we're doing this devotional together. We're learning to spend time with God. We're learning from His Word. Keep it up! You're doing the right thing. It takes a little more time, but it's going to be so good. Just take it one day at a time and we'll get there. I can't wait to see what there is tonight! God saved some sweet surprises for us and tucked them away in His Word. It's up to us to sniff them out and find them. When we do, we're gonna love it. Wow! What a treat! Yum!

Prayer: "Godly Hatred"

I get understanding from your precepts;
therefore, I hate every false path.
Psalm 119:104

God, thank you for caring about me so much that you want me to learn and grow and understand your ways. I know more about you and your ways than I used to when I was a little kid. Lord, I want to know you better, to know your Word better. Please help me. I know you want me to get understanding from your Word. That will help me in my life. Please help me stay focused on your Word. Help me to be faithful to read your Word every day of my life. Help me to put into practice what I learn (James 1:22). That will help me stay away from trouble and off of false paths. I love you, God. In Jesus' name, Amen.

Day 23:

"Light"

Your word is a lamp to my feet and a light for my path.
I have taken an oath and confirmed it,
to keep your righteous judgments.
Psalm 119:105-106

Camp! Juan had been waiting for this night for an entire year! It was the annual scavenger hunt on the first night at camp – in the pitch black dark! He had his bug spray. He had his backpack to gather the treasures he would find based on the clues. He had his packet of clues. There was only one problem. He forgot to pack his flashlight. Mom had told him to go get it and put it in his bag, but he had gotten distracted by his video game. He started out doing okay. There was some light from his cabin, but now he was out among the trees and he didn't even have the moonlight. It was hard to see a path of any kind. The next step could be the one that strays off the path. Now, he was lost in the dark – literally!

Each one of us can be like Juan. We can be going along in life, minding our own business and then, suddenly, we are distracted by something. Before we know it, we can be where we don't know the right way. We can make choices that take us away from the pathway that is right. Sometimes it's easy to choose to do the wrong thing, but that always takes us in a bad direction. It's easy to be selfish and want to choose our own path, to do our own thing, and to go our own way. Those pathways always lead us farther away from God, not closer to God.

Todays' verses remind us that God's Word is a lamp for our feet and a light for our path. You see, God's Word is always pointing the right way. His Word never strays off course. It is *our* feet that wander off the path. When we look to God's Word for wisdom and direction, He always points us in the way of Truth. God's Word always points us to Jesus.

When you realize you are off track – when you need help, look to the Light. It is always pointing you in the right direction. When you're off track, you need to repent – just say, "God, I'm wrong. I blew it. I chose the wrong thing, the wrong way. Please forgive me. Help me to follow You."

It's time for us to get our feet on the right path – walking in the Light. Today is a new day! God gives us a fresh start each morning (Lamentations 3:22-23). Start off today by making an oath or promise to God. Say, "God, I'm going to walk in Your path today, following Your Light." He will help you all along the way. He is the Way! (John 14:6). Let's walk with Him today. Happy trails!

Prayer: "Willing Offering"

I am exceedingly afflicted, Oh Lord,
give me life according to your word.
Accept, Oh Lord, the willing offering of my mouth
and teach me your judgments.
Psalm 119:107-108

Oh, Lord, how great you are! You are awesome, Lord! I am so blessed to have a God like you! You love me with an everlasting love (Jeremiah 31:3). You are my strength (Isaiah 12:2). You are my helper (Psalm 54:4). You are my protector and defender (Psalm 32:7). You are my peace (Micah 5:5). You are Immanuel, God with me (Matthew 1:23). How can I not praise you? Tonight, I lift to you my praises. I love you, O Lord, my God. In Jesus' name, Amen.

Day 24:

"Snare"

My life is in my hands continually,
but I have not forgotten your law.
The wicked have set a snare for me,
but I do not stray from your precepts.
Psalm 119:109-110

Jerod and Ian stopped dead in their tracks. The sign on the path in front of them read, "If you continue along this path, you do so at your own risk – you take your life in your own hands!" What?!? They had just started exploring this part of the jungle. Now, they're getting stopped almost before they had begun. Another sign said, "Snares ahead – BEWARE!" Well, now their imaginations were running wild. Ian wondered aloud, "What does this mean? Steel-jawed traps that will snap off our legs at the knees?" Jerod said, "I'm worried about poison darts that will freeze us like statues." "What about razor sharp knives and whirling blades that will slice off our ears so we can't hear Mom call us to dinner?" mused Ian, "Cause I'm already getting a little hungry. I'm thinking maybe we should turn around now so we don't miss dinner."

Even when we're not venturing through a dense forest or a tropical jungle, all of us have come across people who try to trick us, hurt us, or set traps and snares to mess up our lives. Even the writers of the Bible were treated that way.

David and Jeremiah, to name just two, both mentioned it in their writings (Psalm 141:9; Psalm 142:3; Jeremiah 18:22). Also, we know there were tricksters in Daniel's day. Mean guys set up Daniel by going behind his back to the King so that Daniel would be arrested and thrown into the Lion's Den for simply praying to God.

The Bible tells us that when we choose to follow God, there will be those who will want to be unkind and mistreat us. But Jesus instructed His followers in Matthew 5, that when these things happen we should, "rejoice and be glad, because great is your reward in heaven." He goes on to say, "If someone forces you to go one mile, go with him two miles" (Matthew 5:41), meaning do even more than is asked of you because you are being a witness for Christ.

One thing is very important to remember: while we are out there in the world and we are facing snares and traps that others set to harm us, we are not alone. God has promised to never leave us or forsake us (Joshua 1:5). Also, God specifically tells us he will save us from the snares if we make him our refuge and our fortress (Psalm 91:2-3). So despite the unexpected and hidden snares in our world, will you commit to staying on God's path today? He'll be right there with you. It's the best path to take and you have the promise of the best Companion and Guide. Ready to walk with Him? Let's do it!

Prayer: "My Inheritance"

I have inherited your testimonies forever,
for they are the joy of my heart.
I have inclined my heart to do your statutes,
forever to the end.
Psalm 119:111-112

Thank you, Lord, for today. Thank you that I live in a land where I can read and learn from your Word. That is a huge blessing. Help me to listen and tune in my ears to the message of your Word. As I do that, I will be blessed beyond measure. It will become everlasting riches for me. Your Word is such a vast treasure. I could never spend it all if I tried. Help me to value your Word as the immeasurable treasure it is. Help me to stick with you all the days of my life, loving your Word more day after day. In Jesus' name, Amen.

Day 25:

"Double Minded"

I hate those who are double-minded, but I love your law.
Psalm 119:113

This is a story about Sue. Sue is your friend one day and not your friend the next day. When you and Bekah are playing a computer game, she's friendly and acts like she's your BFF. When Tania is around, Sue acts like she doesn't know you. How do you like being treated that way? Not much fun is it? No, no one really likes it when "friends" do that.

What if I told you I switched the names and it really wasn't a story about 'Sue'. Instead, it is a story about 'you'. What!?! You're thinking, "You must be kidding! I would never really behave that way." I know. I know. None of us really mean to do that. But did you know we sometimes treat God that way? Oops! Didn't see that coming did you? Well, it's true and God doesn't like to be treated that way either. Jesus said, "Love the Lord your God with all your heart and with all your soul and with all your mind and with all your strength" (Mark 12:30). And God said, "You shall have no other gods before me" (Exodus 20:3) and "Fear the LORD your God, serve Him only" (Deuteronomy 6:13).

In the Bible, the Israelites, God's chosen people, went back and forth between following God and then turning away from Him. Many times, they got into a lot of trouble for living that way. God often used their enemies, who attacked, fought and defeated them, to help bring Israel back to their senses. When that happened, Israel would then repent and turn back to God. Now, we certainly don't want that happening to us, so hang on.

You see, God loves you so much He sent His only Son, Jesus, to die for you so that you can have eternal life. God wants to have a very special relationship with you and He has great plans for you (John 3:16; Jeremiah 29:11). In exchange for this, God wants to be Number One in your life – your BFF – forever and forever and forever.

God wants you to love Him – to grow in your relationship with Him by learning and growing in your understanding of His Word and by walking with Him every day (Psalm 86:11). He is constantly looking throughout the whole world to find people who are committed to Him and He promises to help make them strong (2 Chronicles 16:9)! That beats being attacked, fought and defeated by enemy armies any day. So what do you say? Will He find you faithfully walking with Him today?

Prayer: "My Shield"

You are my hiding place and my shield;
I put my hope in your word.
Psalm 119:114

Lord, I have always loved to play hide and seek. It's a fun game. It wouldn't be so fun, though, if I really had to hide from someone to be safe. I know from your Word that there are dangers in the world and that you are my hiding place and my shield to protect me from the evil in this world. Thank you, God. You thought of everything. Now, I know I have somewhere to go, Someone to go to when there are dangers and difficulties. You are the One. You are my Place. I do put all my hope in you and in your Word. Thank you for being there for me, God. I love you. In Jesus' name, Amen.

Day 26:

"Go Away"

Go away from me evildoers, that I may keep the
commandments of my God.
Psalm 119:115

Ainsley loves the two weeks she gets to spend with Grandma every summer. She gets to do things with Grandma that she never does at home. Grandma lives in the country – I mean, way out in the country – where there are no street lights, no fast food restaurants, no movie theaters or shopping malls. They have other things in the country that they don't have where Ainsley lives – things like crickets, cicadas, butterflies, beautiful song birds and, Ainsley's favorite . . . lightning bugs! Every night before bedtime, Ainsley catches a jar full and watches them flicker while she drifts off to sleep.

Today, Ainsley is helping Grandma make apple pies. Whenever Grandma makes pies, she bakes four pies. One is for Mr. Green, whose wife lives in the nursing home. One is for Mrs. Mary, who is raising her three grandchildren. One is for Ms. Williams who lives up on the hill. Ms. Williams doesn't smell very good, but Grandma says they need to be nice to her anyway. And one is for Ainsley and Grandma.

Today, Ainsley's job is to wash the apples. She likes how they bob up and down in the wash tub – floating there like red, rubber duckies. When Grandma finishes slicing one, Ainsley hands her the next one to peel and slice. As Ainsley picks up the next ruby red apple, her finger sinks into a soft, squishy glob of brown mush. "Ewwwww! What's that?" howls Ainsley. "That's just a rotten place on the apple," replies Grandma. "Before we're finished, you'll probably find another one just like it." Ainsley looks puzzled, "Why do you think that, Grandma?" "Often while the apples are at the market sitting on the shelf, as one begins to ruin, those that are touching the rotten spot will begin to rotten, too," Grandma explains. She continues, "Your great grandma used to say, 'One bad apple spoils the whole bunch!'" "That's a funny saying, Grandma," Ainsley giggles. "What was that supposed to mean?" "Well," Grandma continues as she finishes slicing the last yummy apple, "Sometimes she was talking about apples, but usually she was talking with your Aunt Jane and me about our choice of friends. You're going to discover, Little One, that all of us begin to act like the people we spend the most time with. If you hang around with friends who are always helping others, you will develop some habits of being kind and helpful. Your Great Uncle Jimmy went the other way – when he was a teenager, he began to spend time with a bad group of fellas. One day, two of them robbed a gas station and came running out and jumped in Uncle Jimmy's car. Before he could even realize what was happening, the police arrested all of them. His bad choice of friends got him in a lot of trouble. It's like Paul writes in 1 Corinthians, 'Bad company spoils good character' (15:33). So it matters, Ainsley, who you choose for friends. Proverbs 20:11 says, 'Even a child is known by his actions, by whether his conduct is pure and right.' So you need to choose friends who love God and follow His ways and stay away from the bad crowd. Now, let's get these pies in the oven so we can have us a wild game of Crazy 8's!"

Prayer: "Sustain"

Sustain me according to your word and I will live;
do not let me be ashamed from my hope.
Uphold me and I will be delivered; I will look on your
statutes continually.
Psalm 119:116-117

Dear God, thank you for sustaining me, for holding on to me, for helping me. Some days, I don't feel like I could make it without your help. Lord, you hold on to me all the time. Thank you for doing that. Life can be tough as a kid. I want to hold on to you. Help me to keep on believing you and your Word. Help me to keep on trusting you to help me. Help me to keep on telling others about you. Help me to keep on doing the things I'm learning from your Word. Help me to keep on walking with you every day. You are a great God and I love you. In Jesus' name, Amen.

Day 27:

"Discarded"

You reject all who stray from your statutes,
for their deceitfulness is deception.
You discard all of the wicked of the earth like dross;
therefore, I love your testimonies.
Psalm 119:118-119

Imagine this – you come home from school, walk into the kitchen and it's obvious that Mom has been very busy. The best smelling cake in the world is cooling right there in front of you on the counter. You see a fresh batch of marshmallow krispie treats on a bright red platter. With one more sniff, you get a whiff of sweet, juicy strawberries that are sitting beside sunshiny bananas. At the stove, Mom is pouring a bag of chocolate morsels into a pan. You stand there watching those awesome chips of yumminess melt into a smooth river of molten chocolate gooey delight. Mom has planned a fondue party and you're the guest of honor! You can just imagine the tasty delight of sinking the cake, marshmallow krispie treats and luscious fruit and berries into the chocolate and popping it into your mouth. *Ahhhhhhhhhh.*

Okay, let's imagine a different picture now. Instead of Mom using a pan on the stove, let's imagine she has an enormous furnace, larger than your classroom at school. Pretend that the furnace is turned up to 1800 degrees.

Instead of yummy chocolate morsels, imagine she had a giant block of solid silver the size of your bed. When the silver is placed in the furnace at that temperature, it begins to melt. As it melts, it turns from a solid block of silver to molten, liquid silver. The fire is so hot you cannot stand right up beside it like you stood by Mom at the stove, instead, you have to stand back a ways. Now, pretend Mom has on safety goggles, a hard hat and instead of a spoon for stirring, she has a giant spatula-looking thing and she is skimming it across the top of the liquid silver. She rakes the spatula to the edge and you see some "stuff" come over the side of the furnace and drop on the ground. This "stuff" is the impurity that was in the silver – everything that was not "pure silver". When it melted, the impurities rose to the top and were scraped off and thrown in the trash. It was worth nothing – total garbage and would be thrown away and never heard from again.

Now, look back at our Scripture passage for today. The writer of this Psalm is saying all the people who do not follow God's ways – those who reject God's statutes – have chosen deceitfulness and deception. This includes things like gossiping, saying bad things about others, being boastful and proud, doing wrong, disobeying parents and any other sinful thing (Romans 1:29-31). God calls this wickedness and He will discard all the wicked just like the dross that is skimmed off the furnace of silver.

So what should we do in response to today's verses? We should stay away from all wickedness. Instead, we should love God's laws and statutes. We should live our lives for Him. We should follow His ways and love His Word. Then we will make our way prosperous and then we will have great success (Joshua 1:8). That is a much better choice than being skimmed off with a spatula and thrown in the trash. So, let's thank God for His Word and walk with Him today purposing to delight in His Word and to follow Him all the days of our life.

Prayer: "Trembling"

My flesh trembles from fear of you and
I fear your judgments.
Psalm 119:120

Lord, it's no fun to be afraid. I don't like it. When I read this verse, it makes me wonder about what I should fear of you. You are a great and mighty God, all powerful (Deuteronomy 10:17; 2 Chronicles 20:6; Job 12:13; John 13:3; 1 Corinthians 6:14; Revelation 11:17). You show your great might through amazing things like creation and raising Jesus from the dead. Your Word teaches me to show you reverence and honor. I want to honor you with my life, Lord. Help me to line up my life with what I learn from your Word. Teach me to walk in your ways all the days of my life. In Jesus' name, Amen.

Day 28:

"Real"

I have done justice and righteousness;
do not leave me to my oppressors.
Ensure good for your servant;
do not let the arrogant oppress me.
Psalm 119:121-122

"Mom, when are we going to see Uncle Murphy?" called Maisey. "I don't know" Mom called back, "Why?" "Because he sponsored Sheldon and me for the Jump-rope-a-thon and we need to collect what he pledged," Maisey stated. "That's right," chimed in Sheldon, "he needs to pay up!" "You guys are certainly eager beavers on this fundraiser. What's got you so fired up about this one when I couldn't get you to sell a single box of Gooseberry Truffles for the new Senior Citizen Community Center downtown?" asked Mom. "This is to build the new gym at school! We really need one. The old one is like falling down," Maisey stated emphatically while rolling her eyes, "and it is sooooo embarrassing and such a drag." "Yeah" added Sheldon, "the new one's going to be awesome! It's going to have a rock climbing wall, a four-lane bowling alley and exercise bikes! Do you know what that means? NO MORE PUSHUPS! We've got to get this money rollin' in now or we'll be going to Middle School before they ever build the thing. It's the least we can do, really. You know, we really need to leave something behind for the younger kids." "Uh huh," said Mom with a smile, "it's good to see you're so thoughtful about those less fortunate than you."

In this Psalm, the psalmist isn't bragging when he says, "I have done justice and righteousness". He is really counting on the truth of God's Word which says, that if we obey His commands, we can ask God for what we need and He will provide it (1 John 3:21-22). You see, God delights in blessing His children and answering their prayers. Hebrews 4:16 says, "Let us then approach the throne of grace with confidence, so that we may receive mercy and find grace to help us in our time of need." The psalmist was being mistreated by prideful men who wanted to hurt and discredit him, but God was on his side. God is always wanting to bring about justice for His servants, His children, His kids who love Him and want to follow his ways (Luke 18:7-8). God does more than give a pledge or a promise of payment like Uncle Murphy. Rather, God ensures good for His children who trust and obey Him and follow His ways.

So what about you? Wouldn't you love to have the God of the Universe always wanting to bring about justice for you? Would you like someone on your side when prideful, arrogant kids do you wrong? Then, with the psalmist, choose today to do what is just and right. Live according to God's Word and God's ways. Then you can say with the psalmist, "Ensure good for your servant. Do not let the arrogant oppress me" (Psalm 119:122).

Prayer: "According to Your Love"

*My eyes fail for your salvation
and for your righteous word.
Deal with your servant according to your steadfast love
and teach me your statutes.
I am your servant; give me understanding that I might
know your testimonies.*
Psalm 119:123-125

Oh Lord, thank you for your love. I want you to deal with me according to your love. Sometimes I see people dealing with others and it doesn't seem like they are dealing with them according to love. Sometimes I see parents yelling at kids in the store – doesn't seem like love. Sometimes I see teachers dealing with students who did wrong at school – doesn't seem like love. When I do wrong, please deal with me according to your love. I want to learn to change my ways so that I please you. Thank you that your Word teaches me about your love. It is a great kind of love. I love you, too, Lord. In Jesus' name, Amen.

Day 29:

"It is Time"

It is time for you to act, Oh Lord,
they have broken your law.
Psalm 119:126

" I can't believe it's true," as Mom sat down on the sofa bewildered. "Bill just saw it on the six o'clock news. They broke out every light and completely destroyed all the fields" answered Dad. How?" asked Mom. "According to Bill, there were tire tracks from four SUV's and they destroyed the entire soccer complex. We'll have to cancel the tournament," said Dad. Mom said, "But we used all the money in the soccer league's bank account just to get the fields ready. There's no money left for repairs or for cleaning up the mess." "I know. We'll have to tell the kids the entire season is cancelled. As a matter of fact, there will be no more soccer until we can raise enough funds for the repairs," said Dad.

What an outrage! Who would do such a thing? Why would they do it? And, certainly, the lawbreakers should be punished for what they've done! But did you know it happens every day? Yes, people do things they shouldn't do. Laws are broken. And there are always consequences. The police come. Eventually, someone goes to jail. The guilty will be punished. The price has to be paid for all wrongdoing.

In the Bible, God has given us His laws to live by, yet people break His laws on a daily basis. The Bible tells us that God is slow to anger and is overflowing with love. But some day, He will begin to punish those who do wrong and He will not leave the guilty unpunished (Exodus 34:6-7). Now there's some good news and some bad news. If you are receiving God's love and patience, that's good. But it's not going to be good when God begins to do the punishing. That's going to be really bad for those who break God's laws.

So, where do you stand with God? Do you love His Word and try to live by it and keep His laws every day? Or, do you go through your day doing whatever you want, living however you like with no thought of God and His Word? Are you breaking God's laws? One day, God will begin punishing those who break His law. Don't wait for that day. Turn to Jesus today. Ask Him to forgive you. Ask Him to come into your life to be your Savior and Lord. Read His Word. Do what it says (James 1:22). Don't wait another day. Do it right now. Then you can be assured of experiencing God's love and goodness, not his anger. He's waiting for you. Just talk to Him. His ears are listening to you.

Prayer: "Upright"

Therefore, I love your commandments more than gold,
more than fine gold.
Therefore, all of your precepts are upright;
I hate every false path.
Psalm 119:127-128

Teach me, O Lord, to love your commandments more than gold. I don't really care that much about gold right now. I know Mom likes jewelry that's gold. Maybe that's a grown-up thing. I love other stuff – toys, games, clothes, electronics, game systems, sports, tv. Sometimes I spend too much time and energy on these things. At church, I learned that some of these things can become idols to us. I know you don't like that. I don't want to put things before you. I don't want my favorite things to be idols that I value more than you or your Word. Help me grow to love you and your Word more than all other things. It's hard sometimes, but I want you to be first place in my life, Lord. Help me to do it. Help me to live that way every day. In Jesus' name, Amen.

Day 30:

"The Simple"

Your testimonies are wonderful; therefore,
my soul keeps them.
The unfolding of your word gives light,
giving understanding to the simple.
Psalm 119:129-130

"Hey Kaden, whatcha doin'?" "Oh, hey Fritz, I'm playing Simple Sven. It was a free app on my Mom's phone. This little guy, Sven, is trying to reach Sven-topia, which is Level 31, be he keeps doin' things that get him killed. When he bumps into these barrels, he blows up. If he jumps at the wrong time, he falls into this bottomless pit. When he swings on this chain, if he let's go at the wrong time, he goes flying off into space." "That sounds bad," said Fritz, "does he ever win?" Kaden said, with a grunt as Sven plummeted into the pit, "Well, if he eats these green pellets as he goes along, he seems to scoot around some of the problems and get more things right. You just have to watch for them and eat them regularly. Sometimes, you miss a chance to take a jump while Sven is eating one of them, but overall, things seem to go much better when you take the time for Sven to chew them up completely and swallow them. Oh, look, look, look, see, he just chewed up one and now he was able to scoot around that barrel and not blow up!" "Yeah, I saw that," added Fritz. "I don't know what's in those green pellets, but Sven certainly needs to find him some more."

Did you know there are some verses about Simple Sven in the Bible? Well, it doesn't actually say his name, but the Bible talks about those who are "simple". The term, "simple" is used for people who are ignorant and foolish (Proverbs 1:22; 8:5; 14:18). The Bible tells us those people who are ignorant and foolish live lives that are completely full of bad choices and awful consequences (Proverbs 14:15; 14:18; 22:3; 1:32). It's not like these folks are not smart enough, nor did they necessarily make bad grades in school. Instead, they just don't take the time to read and learn from God's Word. They live a life of making up their own rules and following their own way. They don't know or acknowledge God or His laws. They're just like Sven, going through life bumping into situations that blow up. They make a bad choice and have a terrible fall. Maybe that terrible fall involves losing an important relationship. Maybe they chose to cheat and wound up bumping into the teacher, or worse yet, the police. And those are small things. As people grow up, the bumps and the consequences get bigger and bigger.

So what helped Sven to have victory over his circumstances? Taking time to find the green pellets, chew them up and swallow them. So, how does that apply to us? Well, God's Word, His laws and His promises are like those green pellets. We simply have to take the time, every day, to sit down with God's Word, read it, think about it, pray and ask Him to help us understand it and do what it says. When we do that regularly, over time, God gives to us His wisdom. He helps us to be wise about what is good and innocent of what is evil (Romans 16:19). The more time we spend in God's Word with Jesus, who is the light of the world (John

8:12), the more we are able to walk in the light as He is in the light (1 John 1:7). Psalm 92:5-7 NIrV says, "Lord, how great are the things you do! How wise your thoughts are! Here is something a man who isn't wise doesn't know. Here is what a foolish person doesn't understand. Those who are evil spring up like grass. Those who do wrong succeed. But they will be destroyed forever." So, make sure you are wiser than Sven. Find those important things in God's Word today. Take God's truths into your life, scoot around some of life's problems by using the wisdom you gain from God's Word and burst forth in victory every day!

Prayer: "Panting"

I open wide my mouth and pant,
for I long for your commandments.
Psalm 119:131

Lord, I don't think I've ever panted for commandments. That seems weird to me. My dog pants when he's hot and thirsty and needs a drink. I guess he really needs water. Now that I think about it, I do really need your Word. I know I need to know what it says. I know your Word teaches me how to live (2 Timothy 3:16). I know it helps make me wise for salvation (2 Timothy 3:15). I know I need your forgiveness. I need your love. I need your help. I need the companionship of your Holy Spirit. I need you in my life. I find all of this in your Word, Lord. I guess I really do need your Word like my dog needs water on a hot day. Your Word is necessary for life. I guess it's not so weird to pant for the commandments in your Word, after all. Thank you, God, for teaching me from your Word. I pant for you. In Jesus' name, Amen.

Day 31:

"Established"

Turn to me and be gracious, as is fitting
for those who love your name.
Establish my footsteps in your word,
and do not let any iniquity rule over me.
Redeem me from the oppression of men that
I may keep your precepts.
Psalm 119:132-134

It was still dark outside when Lani got up from her mat, rolled it up and put it in the corner. Quickly and quietly, she picked up her basket and slipped out the door of the filthy hovel she lived in to begin her chores. It was always best to be unseen and unheard. Anyone who drew attention to herself paid a price for it later. Her owner was a hard man. His punishments were harsh, often leaving marks. Some of the marks never went away.

Lani's mother had died after contracting malaria and her owner had denied her any treatment. Two of Lani's cousins belonged to this man, too. Koutze, the older of the two sisters, was crippled now after being beaten severely because she did not collect as many eggs as the master thought she should have brought to him. So Lani worked hard. She knew she had to work hard every day of her life if she wanted to live.

Unknown to Lani, a man who owned much land and

many herds came to Lani's owner and offered to purchase Lani. At first, Lani's owner did not want to part with Lani because she was a hard worker, but Lani's owner was greedy. The man who wanted to purchase Lani offered an unheard of price – more than Lani's owner had ever seen before. He could not withstand his greedy impulses so he sold Lani to the man.

At first, Lani was scared of the stranger. She was afraid he would be a harsh taskmaster. He could have been even worse than the evil man who owned her from the start. But this new man had a kind face. He smiled at her as they walked home. He had a kind voice and told her many things she had not heard before. When they reached his home, she could not believe her eyes. This was not a filthy, rat-infested dump like her previous home. This was the most beautiful mansion she had ever seen. And now, she could not believe what she was hearing. This man had purchased her to grant her freedom. She was no longer a slave. He wanted her to be his child, an heir to all that was before her. How could this be? She was a poor slave girl with nothing to offer, yet this man was offering her everything!

You and I are in the same situation as Lani. The Bible says that we were slaves to sin (Romans 6:17). It teaches us that while we were still sinners, Christ died for us (Romans 5:8). The Bible says that we are purchased by His blood (1 Peter 1:18-19). And because of what Jesus did on the cross, we can be joint heirs with Christ (Romans 8:17). All we have to do is choose to trust Jesus as our Savior, turn from our sins and turn to Him. We need to pray a simple prayer like this: *"Jesus I believe you are the Son of God and that you died on the cross to take the punishment for the wrong things I have done. Please forgive me of my sin, come into my life, and be my Savior and Lord."* It's that simple. Right now, you can choose to no longer be a slave to sin. You can be set free! Would you like to be free? Let go of what is holding you back and pray to Jesus right now. He's already paid the price. He's ready to set you free. Talk to Him right now.

Prayer: "Learning to Weep"

*Cause your face to shine on your servant
and teach me your statutes.
Streams of tears pour from my eyes because
they have not kept your law.*
Psalm 119:135-136

Lord, I love sunshiny days when the warm light kisses my face and makes me smile. I like thinking about you smiling down on me, too. Because I know you love me, I want to know your ways. Teach me from your Word and help me walk in your ways. Help me grow to be more and more like you. I know it makes you sad when you see people not following your ways. I need to notice when people are not following your ways. Help me to do that, Lord. And, help me to learn to see things the way you see them. So when you see wrongdoing, help me realize it is wrongdoing. When you see evil, help me realize it is evil, too. I pray that other people will follow you because they see me following you. I pray in Jesus' name, Amen.

Day 32:

"Tested"

You are righteous, Oh Lord,
and your judgments are upright.
You have commanded your testimonies in righteousness
and in exceeding faithfulness.
My zeal consumes me, for my enemies
have forgotten your words.
Your word has been tested exceedingly
and your servant loves it.
Psalm 119:137-140

"Mom, Binti told me today she can't come with me to my World Missions class. Mrs. Denise told us to invite our friends and Binti is my best friend so I invited her but she says her parents won't let her come." "Did she say why they won't let her come," Mom asked Ella. "She said her family doesn't believe in God. Instead, they worship something-or-other that I've never heard of and she said that the Bible's not true. How could she say that? What does that even mean, 'the Bible's not true?'?"

"Well, Ella," Mom continued, "unfortunately, there are people in the world who don't believe in the one, true God. And, they don't believe His Word. Sadly, Binti's family falls in that group of people." Ella thought for a moment then said, "How do we know what we believe about God and the Bible is true and Binti's family is wrong?"

"That's a good question, Ella. There are several ways we know that. First, the truth of the Bible is well documented in hundreds of ways throughout history. The events recorded in the Bible were documented by historians for hundreds, even thousands of years. So if we wanted, or needed to, we could go and find evidence of people, places, things and events the Bible tells us about in history books all over the world. But the most important way we know is that your dad and I have both experienced God's amazing work in our own lives after we trusted Him as our Savior. We talk to Him each day and He speaks to us through His Word, through prayer, through other believers and through circumstances. He's made a huge difference in our lives and we'll never be the same. Now, we have the assurance of a home with Him forever. Binti's family doesn't have any of that."

"Oh, that's so sad for them," added Ella, "what can we do?" "We can pray for them," Mom said, "that they will open their hearts and minds to the truth of the Gospel and that the light of God's Word will penetrate the darkness they live in. Also, you can be a good, kind friend to Binti so that she sees Jesus living in you." "Could we bake them some cookies?" asked Ella. "Sure," said Mom. "How about right now? We can pray for them while we bake! Let's do it!"

Prayer: "Despised"

I am small and despised;
I have not forgotten your precepts.
Your righteousness is an eternal righteousness
and your law is true.
Distress and anguish have found me;
your commandments are my delight.
Your testimonies are righteous for eternity;
give me understanding that I may live.
Psalm 119:141-144

Dear Lord, you know I'm still pretty young, but I know some stuff about you. I know you are good. And I know some of what the Bible teaches. I'm learning more of it all the time. I know you are forever and you're preparing a place for me that is forever (John 14:2). I know your Word is true (Psalm 33:4). Lord, please help me to keep learning your Word and your ways. Help me to live for you all the days of my life. Help me follow you. Help my life count for you. You are a good God. You are my good God. And I'm yours. In Jesus' name, Amen.

Day 33:

"Crying Out"

I call with all of my heart; answer me,
Oh Lord, and I will keep your statutes.
I call out to you; save me and I will
keep your testimonies.
I rise early in the morning and I cry for help;
I have put my hope in your word.
Psalm 119:145-147

A'Nelli stood in the street screaming. Her little sister, Seri, had just been killed in a fight between rival gang members in her small village. A'Nelli screamed for someone to help her, but no one stopped. They just hurried on by. She looked for someone who cared, but no one came. Everyone was afraid of the gangs, so no one would get involved. There was no police force in her small village, really. There were some old officers, but they were afraid to do anything because the gangs had threatened their families. Would no one help A'Nelli?

Do you have troubles sometimes? Do you have people who will help you with your troubles? Most likely you have some people in your life who care about you and will help you when problems come along. If so, thank God for those people. We are blessed when we have people who care.

But, what about problems and troubles and worries you have kept as a secret inside you? You know, those you haven't told anyone about and you don't want to tell anyone about them. What about those? Do you think anyone cares about those? The person who wrote this psalm says in today's verses that when he has those big worries, he calls out to God. With all his heart, in extreme passion and concern, he cries out to God to save him and help him. Because the psalmist loved God's Word and kept God's commands, he was assured of God's help.

That same assurance is available to us. Psalm 18:3 KJV says, "I will call upon the Lord, who is worthy to be praised. So shall I be saved from my enemies." God also tells us in Jeremiah 29:12-13 to call on Him and He will answer. When we look for Him, we'll find Him. He's not hiding. He wants us to come to Him. The New Testament tells us the same thing. We need to cast all our worries on Him because He cares for us (1 Peter 5:7). The prophet, Nahum, said, "The LORD is good, a refuge in times of trouble. He cares for those who trust in Him" (Nahum 1:7). Another Old Testament prophet, Zephaniah, says, "The LORD your God is with you. He is mighty enough to save you. He will take great delight in you. The quietness of His love will calm you down. He will sing with joy because of you" (Zephaniah 3:17 NIrV).

There are many, many more verses where God tells us how much he loves and cares for us. He wants to take care of us. We just need to trust Him and follow His guidelines that we find in His Word. Whenever you have troubles and worries you can always go to God. God cares for you and He cares for A'Nelli. Do you know some kids, like A'Nelli, who don't have anyone who loves them and helps take care of them? Stop and pray for those kids right now. Maybe God wants you to be the one to let them know how much

He loves them and wants to help them. Don't let those kids stand there alone in the world thinking no one cares. You can show your love and care by sharing these verses with them and letting them know how much God cares for them. How about today?

Prayer: "Night Watches"

My eyes anticipate the night watches,
to meditate on your word.
Psalm 119:148

Thank you, Lord, for today. It was a busy day and I'm a little tired now. As I lay down to go to sleep, help my thoughts be of you. Help me to remember how good you've been to me and lead me to praise you. Help me to remember those things you've taught me and remind me to thank you. Help me to remember how strong and mighty you are and remind me to trust you. Thank you that you can teach me in the daytime or in the nighttime. Thank you for always being with me. I love you, Lord, in Jesus' name, Amen.

Day 34:

"Far"

Hear my voice according to your steadfast love,
Oh Lord, give me life according to your judgments.
Those who pursue evil draw near;
they are far from your law.
Psalm 119:149-150

Franklin crouched behind a cardboard box. He thought he had lost his pursuers. He slowed his breathing and listened carefully for any footsteps crunching through the grass. Hearing nothing, he quietly raised his head above the edge of the box and *WHAPPP!!!!* Very Berry Blueberry frosting was dripping out of his curly red hair. Giggles erupted from the culprits. Now that he was hit, he stood up to unleash his Lemon Raspberry cupcake revenge on his foe. However when he stood, eight more heavily frosted bakery delights pelted him from every side at close range – he was surrounded and he never even knew they were there. Now Franklin looked like a heavily frosted cupcake himself – with curly red hair on top!

Today's verses tell us that those who do evil are nearby – much like the cupcake bombers were circled around Franklin. You probably even know some of the evil dudes who are nearby, but maybe you don't think of them as evil-doers. It could be that some of them are even your friends. Uhhhh, so, you don't think you know any of them, huh?

Okay, maybe not, but have you heard anyone use God's name as part of a curse word? Do you know anyone who has ever lied? What about someone who took something that didn't belong to him? Hmmm, do you know anyone who wants, wishes, and longs to have their friends' clothes, game system, phone, computer, pool or vacation? (That's called coveting.)

Those are just a few of the things God calls evil. It's really sad but, sometimes those of us who are Christians can act that way, too. So what would cause that? How could that be? The Bible says that we can't be close to God if we're not close to His Word. We need to spend time reading God's Word, meditating on it, memorizing it, singing it, and making it a part of our everyday lives. When we do, we won't find ourselves on God's list of evil-doers.

In Matthew 7:1-5, Jesus said something like: *Don't worry so much about the cupcake frosting in someone else's hair when you've got frosting dripping from your curls, your ears, your nose and your elbow.* Pursue Christ. Make sure you spend time in God's Word every day. Call out to Him. Walk with Him. Make Him the center of your life. Then, you will stay far away from evil.

Prayer: "Near"

You are near, Oh Lord, and all of your
commandments are true.
Long ago I have known from your testimonies that you
established them for eternity.
Psalm 119:151-152

Wow, Lord, I'm glad you're near. When I look up at the stars in the sky, it seems like you would be far away, beyond the stars, but this verse says you are near to me. I like that. When I'm afraid, I like for you to be near. When I don't know what to do, I like for you to be near. You know, God, it's nice being near someone who loves you. I know you love me because of your goodness to me, because of your mercy and because you allowed Jesus to go to the cross in my place. I really know you love me. It's very nice to have you near. Help me remember you are near me all the time, whether I'm scared or happy or sad or whatever. You are near and that's good for me. Thank you, God. In Jesus' name, Amen.

Day 35:

"Contending"

Look upon my affliction and deliver me,
for I have not forgotten your law.
Plead my cause and redeem me;
give me life according to your word.
Psalm 119:153-154

Howie was an inventor. He loved to tinker and build things. His favorite store was the Resale Shop on the corner. He could get great stuff there for really cheap. As soon as he got his hot deals home, he would disassemble them and create some totally new gizmo that he said would "revolutionize the world!" He could picture himself as a gazillionaire before he was twelve years old.

His most amazing invention, so far, came as quite a shock to most of the bullies in the neighborhood who thrived on picking on "the little nerdy inventor." This great new gizmo looked like an ordinary bicycle horn with a strange cord attached. Of course, each bully he came upon would see Howie carrying his little contraption and the bully couldn't stand to let the golden opportunity pass without saying something like, "Hey Einstein, what's up with the bicycle horn? Did you lose your bicycle?" On cue, Howie would honk the horn, and, to everyone's surprise, a cherry red boxing glove on a giant spring would bounce out of Howie's backpack and bop the bully right on the nose.

While the bully was still seeing stars, Howie would strut down the street, confident he had made the world a safer place for nerds everywhere.

Some days, I really wish I had one of Howie's bop-o-matic gizmos. I think I could use one. There are times when I have people bugging me and bothering me and messing with me and I really wish I could just bop somebody! How about you? Do you ever have days like that? In today's verses, the writer of this Psalm says to God, "Look upon my affliction and deliver me." He's saying, "God, look at my troubles. Come and take up for me because I have not forgotten your law."

It seems like it would be great if we could honk a horn and *–ZING!! –* God would be there to bop people who are bothering us, but that's not what this verse is saying. It really means when we are standing up for what is right and just and holy, and when we are being a witness for God and *then* we are mistreated, then God will come and defend us. Jesus will tell God how happy He is for how we are standing for Him (Matthew 10:32-33). When we act foolishly and bear the consequences of our own foolish behavior, we can't expect God to send lightning bolts from the sky to zap our foes. Hmmm, seems like we should be careful about what we say and what we do. I don't have a backpack and a bopper. I think I'll just stick close to God and His Word. How about you?

Prayer: "Far from the wicked"

Salvation is far from the wicked,
for they do not seek your statutes.
Psalm 119:155

Lord, I know some people who are far from you. I can tell by the way they live and the things they do, they aren't living according to your Word. Some of them do mean things. Some of them cheat and steal and lie. Lord, I know you don't approve of those things. Please help those people come to you. Help them to learn about your Word and your ways. Help them to begin to follow you. Help me to tell them about you, how much you mean to me and how awesome you really are. They don't know and they need to know. I pray they will listen to you starting tonight. In Jesus' name, Amen.

Day 36:

"Many Compassions"

Your compassions are many, Oh Lord;
give me life according to your judgments.
My persecutors and my distress are many; I have not
turned from your testimonies.
Psalm 119:156-157

Once upon a time, there was a kingdom. It was the most beautiful kingdom in all the land. It stretched from beyond the farthest snowcapped mountain peaks to the warm sandy beaches that hugged the rolling sea. Throughout this kingdom, the subjects thrived, living happy, contented lives because their king was honorable and loving and ruled his kingdom with justice and compassion.

Outside this kingdom were other kingdoms. None so happy as this one, though. The other kings were neither honorable, loving nor just. As a result, their subjects were dishonest and evil and often sought to destroy the good king and his people.

One day, as the good king walked among his people, some of his guards brought one of his subjects to him. The man was bruised and beaten. He was so weak, he couldn't walk and could barely speak. The king had his guards take the man to the castle. The king, himself, bandaged his wounds, held his head in his lap and helped him take some food and drink. He listened to the man's story, sent his guards to find and deal with the evil intruders from the other lands and then gave him a safe place with a warm bed where he could rest and recover.

These were the actions of the honorable and loving king who ruled his kingdom with justice and compassion.

Our God is the Lord of lords and the King of kings (Revelation 17:14). He is the Alpha and the Omega, the Beginning and the End (Revelation 21:6). He gave His one and only Son, Jesus, that whoever believes in Him will have eternal life (John 3:16). Because, you see, God is love (1 John 4:8) and He doesn't want anyone to be without Jesus (2 Peter 3:9). God is overflowing with love for you (Exodus 34:6). And, He is full of compassion (Psalm 116:5) – loving care and concern. As a matter of fact, it is because of the Lord's great love for us that we're able to keep going. And the best part is, this loving care (compassion) and His great mercies (sparing us from what we really deserve) come fresh and new every morning. No matter how much love and mercy He gave us yesterday, our loving King has a new batch of love and mercy ready for us each new day (Lamentations 3:21-23).

These are the actions of our loving, compassionate and merciful God and King. And that makes me break forth in praise – Hallelujah!

Prayer: "All"

*I look on the faithless and I loathe them because
they do not keep your word.
See that I love your precepts; Oh Lord, give me life
according to your steadfast love.
All of your words are true and all of your righteous
judgments are eternal.*
Psalm 119:158-160

*Last night, Lord, we talked about those people who are
far from you, who don't know you and your ways. I'm still
thinking about them tonight because I know they are on the
wrong path. Lord, I'm trying to stay on your path and learn
to do things your way. Help me to keep loving you and
walking with you and doing what is right. Don't let me be
influenced to do wrong by those who aren't living for you.
Instead, let them see how you've changed me and let them
begin following you. Your Word is true and right. Help me
to follow you all the days of my life. In Jesus' name, Amen.*

Day 37:

"Deception"

Rulers persecute me without cause,
but my heart trembles at your word.
I rejoice over your words as one who finds great riches.
I hate and abhor deception, but I love your law.
Psalm 119:161-163

Walking toward you down the hallway, you see a lanky figure. You look again and see it is Lucinda, or as her fellow students refer to her, Lying Lulu. It's not that Lucinda set out to be known as a liar. It's just that she discovered that when she changed the way she told things, it got her out of some trouble. It started out small. You know, when her teacher said, "Where is your homework?" Lucinda would say, "I lost it." Surprisingly, her teacher believed her and gave her another chance to turn it in the next day. Another time, when Allee told her she liked her boots, Luci said, "Oh, these old things? I got them at the Chic Boutique," when she really got them at the Used Shoe Outlet. Then there was the time Lulu told one group of kids her dad was a secret agent. She told another bunch he worked for the Homeland Security. He really worked as an overnight security guard at a storage unit place.

Have you ever known a person who lies? Have you known someone who told lies and never seemed to get caught? It was almost like the more they lied, the better things went for them. It would almost be easy to envy someone who seems to have everything going their way – even if they had to lie to do it. Lucinda decided if she 'bent' the truth just a little, no one would get hurt, it helped her look better to her classmates and, besides, who would ever find out?

But, how do you think Luci will look when her teacher stops believing her? What will her classmates say when someone sees her dad dropping her off at school in his security guard uniform? It is possible that no one at school will find out, but there is someone who knows all things. That's right – God. In His Word, He tells us what He thinks about those who deceive others.

First of all, "Thou shalt not lie" is on the *Top Ten List* He gave to Moses and He wrote it in stone (Exodus 20:16)! I think that makes it pretty important. In Proverbs 17:20, we discover that those who deceive others will not prosper. Also, Ephesians 5:6 tells us that God's anger is coming on those who deceive. And don't forget about what Psalm 37:1-3 says – "Do not fret because of evil men or be envious of those who do wrong; for like the grass they will soon wither, like green plants they will soon die away. Trust in the LORD and do good." So, you see, it never really works out well for those who lie.

And what about you? Do you ever think about lying? Ever try it out? According to God's Word, lying is sin and we should never do it. The Good News is that Jesus came to provide forgiveness for sin. When you sin, confess it to Jesus and ask Him to forgive you. Learn to hate what is evil. Cling to what is good (Romans 12:9). Learn to value God's Word as much as you would treasures of gold or precious jewels – that will never get you into trouble and God will bless you abundantly for loving His Word and living by His truth. So, you say, "What about Lulu?" Well, she's on the path to destruction. "Truthful lips endure forever, but a lying tongue lasts only a moment" (Proverbs 12:19).

Prayer: "Great Peace"

*Seven times in the day I praise you
for your righteous judgments.
Great peace have those who love your law and nothing
makes them stumble.*
Psalm 119:164-165

Lord, I like having great peace. I don't like it when there is fussing and fighting and Mom gets irritated. That means no peace for anybody. I also really don't like it when I trip and stumble and fall and skin my knee. This verse says that you give peace to people who love your ways and somehow you keep them from stumbling and falling. I like that. I know your Word helps me have peace in my life when I make right choices and do the right things. Things just work out better when I do that. Thank you for your peace and thank you for Jesus, your Son, who is the Prince of Peace. I wonder if that makes you the King of Peace. Hmm, could be. Well, good night, God. I love you and I pray in Jesus' name, Amen.

Day 38:

"Waiting"

I wait for your salvation, Oh Lord,
and I do your commandments.
My soul keeps your testimonies
and I love them exceedingly.
Psalm 119:166-167

Marna knew the reality of having her hopes crushed. She lived, every day, in a dark, filthy prison. The worst part was she hadn't done anything wrong. She was completely innocent. Someone had blamed her for something she didn't do, and then others lied to insure she would go to prison. And she wasn't alone. There were many others in that same prison who were innocent, as well. But Marna had noticed something interesting. While several like her were innocent, they didn't all act the same. Most of them were angry and bitter. As time wore on, they became filled with hate and always sought revenge.

Marna, on the other hand, was able to rise above that, you see, Marna had trusted Jesus as her Savior. She had the Holy Spirit living in her (Romans 8:9). God had given her a gift for her to use every day (Romans 12:4-8).

Marna decided early on that she couldn't do anything about *where* she was, but she could do something about her attitude and *how* she behaved. So, while she waited and prayed for her release, she made up her mind to be kind, sweet, gentle and to seek Christ first each day (Matthew 6:33), to keep her mind focused on Him (Isaiah 26:3) and to use her gifts to serve others who needed to know of God's love.

Just like Marna, many are held captive by different things and everyone is waiting for something – for Christmas vacation, for summer to come, to be in the seventh grade, for Dad to come pick you up. And just like Marna, we have a choice about our attitude and *how* we will behave. We can be angry, resentful and bitter or we can trust God, seek Him in His Word and keep our mind focused on Him. That's what He wants us to do.

So what have you been choosing lately? Have you been angry, bitter or resentful? Or, have you been kind, sweet and gentle while serving others and following after God? And what will you choose for today? Choose not to waste your time and your life on anger, resentment and bitterness. Choose love, joy, peace, patience, kindness, goodness, faithfulness, gentleness and self-control (Galatians 5:22-23). You do that by trusting Jesus as your Savior and then by spending time in His Word every day. While you're waiting, choose God.

Prayer: "Known to You"

I keep your precepts and your testimonies, for all of my ways are before you.
Psalm 119:168

Okay, God, we need to talk about this. I do try to keep your laws, Lord, and follow your commands. And, I know that you know all things, but sometimes I may forget that you're watching ALL the time. So now that I'm thinking about this, I'm pretty sure you know that I mess up some and don't get it all right, like today when I _____. I'm sorry God. Please forgive me. Help me start clean tomorrow and remember to do right all day long. Thank you for your forgiveness. You are so good to me. I love you. In Jesus' name, Amen.

Day 39:

"Lips"

May my cry reach you, Oh Lord; give me
understanding according to your word.
May my supplication come before you;
deliver me according to your word.
My lips will pour out praise, for you have
taught me your statutes.
My tongue will sing of your word, for all of
your commandments are righteous.
Psalm 119:169-172

Deep in the pristine forest of Belwyn was a secluded, wooded glen. Even in the extreme heat of summer, it was cool and refreshing because of the shade of the ancient trees. Soft light filtered down through the branches with patches of golden sunlight that glistened like spotlights on a darkened stage.

Because this area was so secluded, it was filled with plant and animal life not seen in any other part of the world. This glen was also inhabited by a colony of Fiddledees. These little creatures stood no more than two feet tall. They were fast and agile, very animated and very, very opinionated. Since each one valued his opinion so highly, often you would find all of them chattering at the same time. When they were all speaking at once, the noise broke the pristine

silence of the peaceful forest and sounded something like a busy street corner at rush hour!

Besides being only two feet tall and all speaking at the same time, the Fiddledees had another quirk – as they spoke, their lips changed color! Take Fwip, for example. Fwip was a happy, helpful Fiddledee. If you sneaked up on him and listened to his conversations, you would almost always hear him encouraging others, singing happy songs and, generally, sharing kindness through his words to the other Fiddledees. As Fwip would talk and sing, his lips fluoresced the most beautiful hues of pink and purple flowers, yellow sunshine and peachy-orange cantaloupe. Fwop, on the other hand, could be overheard using his words to grumble, complain, whine, fuss and blame other Fiddledees for everything from the dew on his toadstool to the bump in his hollow log. Interestingly, as he spoke, his lips glowed shades of murky green stagnant algae to the dirty brown of a giant Wooly Woop's stinky, plop patty. All in all, considering the Fiddledees words, they were a colorful group!

Now, let's think about your words. Do you use your words to encourage, help and share kindness or do your words sound like grumbling, complaining, whining, fussing and blaming? In Isaiah 29:13 we read, "The Lord says: 'These people come near to me with their mouth and honor me with their lips, but their hearts are far from me.'" God wants our words to honor Him and He wants us to show that we belong to him by how we live. In today's verses, the psalmist used his words to praise God because of the blessing we receive from God's Word. He called out to God, asking God to help him understand God's Word and then deliver him when he faced troubles. Psalm 105:1-3 says we should praise God and make Him known to all people. Hebrews 3:13 reminds us we should use our words to encourage others. Colossians 4:6 helps us remember the goal is to use our words to bring out the best in others, not to put them down. So as you think about the past few days, what color have your lips been? What color will they be today?

Prayer: "Your Hand"

May your hand help me, for I have chosen your precepts.
Psalm 119:173

Lord, I'm glad about your hands. I have chosen your ways and to follow your truths. I'm glad you're right here to help me and I have your hand to guide me. It's like when I was really little and I would hold onto Mom or Dad's hand when I was learning to walk. When I was unsteady and wasn't sure I could do it, they would hold onto me. Then, they would let me take a few little steps by myself. Thank you for helping me learn to walk with you. Thank you for guiding me, for making me steady when I'm not sure which way to go or what to do. It's good to have your hands here to help me. Thank you, God. In Jesus' name, Amen.

Day 40:

"And I Will Praise"

I long for your salvation, Oh Lord,
and I meditate on your law.
May my soul live and I will praise you, and may your
judgments help me.
Psalm 119:174-175

Sally stared out the window, oblivious to the chaos her younger brothers were creating around her as they acted out the final battle scene between the aliens and the dinosaurs. Sally was looking past the busy street, above the neighboring apartment building, beyond the billboard, through the clouds. She didn't even hear Mom call her for dinner. Yancey had to punch her to snap her out of it. "Hey, why did you hit me?" protested Sally. "Mom said 'Come to dinner'," shouted Yancey over his shoulder down the hall. "What were you looking at anyway?" asked Yancey as he passed her the bowl of corn. "Nothing really. I was just thinking about what Mrs. Kay said in my class on Sunday. She had asked how she could pray for us this week and I told her about the report I have to do in class on Tuesday and how nervous I get. She said she would pray for me, but I should also read Philippians 4:13 NLT and meditate on that. I looked that verse up and it says, 'I can do everything through Christ, who gives me strength.' I've been thinking about it, but I'm not really sure how just thinking about it is going to help me with my report."

Mom chimed in, "Psalm 119:174-175 tells us 'I long for your salvation, Oh Lord, and I meditate on your law. May my soul live and I will praise you, and may your judgments help me.' Meditating is not just mindlessly staring out the window. It is actively thinking about God's Word and what it means and how to go about obeying what we discover in God's Word. It is digging into God's Word and finding other truths that go along with the one Mrs. Kay told you about on Sunday. It is learning God's Word, memorizing God's Word, praying God's Word and practicing living it out while we wait on God to answer our prayer for His help. So, Sally, as you see God helping you with your report, then your job is to burst out in praise to God for helping you through your difficult situation. Meditation, prayer, struggle and learning should always lead us back to praise."

Like Sally, we all face struggles in life. Often as we read God's Word, we find a nugget of truth tucked in a passage that fits our situation. Our job is to take that truth, pray that God will help us learn that truth and apply it to our lives. While we are waiting on God to act – to answer our prayer – we continue to think on that truth and read His Word daily. He will show us other truths that work together with that truth. As we watch and wait, pray and think, we should continue to dig into God's Word. When we see God begin to answer our prayers to Him, to help us with the things we need, we should break out in an explosion of thanks and praise to God for hearing and answering our prayers. He is our AWESOME GOD and every day we need to be people of praise!

Prayer: "Lost Sheep"

*I have strayed as a lost sheep; seek your servant
because I have not forgotten your commandments.*
Psalm 119:176

*Lord, I admit that sometimes I stray off the right path.
Sometimes, it's an accident – I didn't really mean to do it.
Other times, I confess I did think about it and I chose to
do wrong. Please forgive me. Lord, I don't want to get off
your path. I don't want to wander far away from you. That
would be scary and I know bad things can happen when
I choose to do wrong. Help me to always remember your
commands. Help me to always walk with you and stay on
the right path. Help me to grow stronger in you and be
more and more committed to your Word and your ways.
Help me to follow you when I'm a kid and help me to still
be following you when I'm a grown-up. You are the One,
true God and I want to walk with you all the days of my life.
I'll be looking for you in your Word in the morning, talking
with you throughout the day and resting in you tomorrow
night, too. I love you, Lord, and pray in Jesus' name, Amen.*

CPSIA information can be obtained
at www.ICGtesting.com
Printed in the USA
FSOW03n1538190816
23980FS

9 781498 470025